# BULIMIA

# BULIMIA

*A Guide
for Family and Friends*

ROBERTA TRATTNER SHERMAN

RON A. THOMPSON

Jossey-Bass Publishers • San Francisco

Substantial discounts on bulk quantities of Jossey-Bass books
are available to corporations, professional associations, and
other organizations. For details and discount information,
contact the special sales department at Jossey-Bass Inc.,
Publishers (415) 433-1740; Fax (800) 605-2665.

For sales outside the United States, please contact
your local Simon & Schuster International Office

Jossey-Bass Web address: http://www.josseybass.com

Printed in the United States of America

*Library of Congress Cataloging-in-Publication Data*

Sherman, Roberta Trattner, date.
Bulimia : a guide for family and friends / Roberta Trattner
Sherman, Ron A. Thompson.
p.   cm. — (The Jossey-Bass psychology series)
Originally published: Lexington, Mass. : Lexington Books,  1990.
Includes bibliographical references and index.
ISBN 0-7879-0361-2 (pb)
1. Bulimia—Popular works.  I. Thompson, Ron A.  II. Title.
III. Series.
RC552.B84S484   1997
616.85'263—dc21                                                              96-45095

HB Printing   10 9 8 7 6 5 4 3
PB Printing   10 9 8 7 6 5 4 3 2

*to*

BONNIE, JEFFREY, AND ALLISON

# Contents

## PART IV
# Treatment

# Acknowledgments

W E wish to thank the many people who helped make this book possible. Just as this book focuses on the importance and value of family and friends as powerful positive influences in an individual's life, we would like to acknowledge and thank those many family members and friends who have been encouraging and supportive, not only with regard to this book but throughout our lives.

More specifically, we wish to thank Jim Sherman, Bonnie Sherman, and two anonymous reviewers for their helpful comments on earlier drafts of this book. We also wish to thank those patients and their families who made valuable suggestions on segments of this book.

Most of all, we wish to thank our patients who taught us not only about eating disorders but also, more important, about the people who have them.

PART

I

## Introduction

Bulimia is a very complex and serious disorder that is a source of anxiety and concern not only for the bulimic individuals themselves but also for those who care most about them—their families and friends. Although this book contains information that could be helpful to bulimic people, it is in no way intended to be a substitute for treatment. Recovery from bulimia typically requires a multidimensional treatment approach provided by mental health practitioners experienced in treatment of eating disorders. Such an approach is well beyond the scope and purpose of this book. The purpose of this book is simply to serve as a guide for the families and friends of bulimics in their attempts to better understand the disorder and to assist in overcoming it.

This book is arranged in a question and answer format. The questions are those most often asked by the families and friends of the hundreds of bulimic patients with whom we have worked. We have attempted to provide answers that are informative as well as practical. Topics have been divided into nine chapters and clustered into four parts. This first part is an overview of bulimia and presents aspects of the disorder that will be developed more extensively in subsequent chapters.

Throughout the book, patient examples are provided to explain and illustrate salient aspects of bulimia. Although all critical information is extracted from actual cases, names and other possible indentifying information have been changed to protect the privacy and confidentiality of our patients. Finally, feminine pronouns—"she," "her," and "herself"—were employed throughout the book primarily because most of the individuals with bulimia are female and also because we wished to avoid the cumbersome use of "he/she," "his/her," and "himself/herself."

# 1

# Overview

## What Is Bulimia?

Bulimia, or more technically, bulimia nervosa, is an eating disorder characterized by episodes of binge-eating that are usually followed by a purging process. Typically, binge episodes consist of eating large quantities of food—often food high in calories. Generally, this eating is done secretively and can occur for years without others being aware of it. Purging most frequently occurs through self-induced vomiting, but may also include laxative abuse, diuretic (water-pill) abuse, fasting, and excessive exercise.

The purpose of the purging is to "undo" the binge. It is an attempt to relieve the guilt of the binge-eating and to minimize any weight gain that might ordinarily take place as a result of binge-eating. Purging is probably more destructive than bingeing for two reasons. First, there are many more physical and medical dangers associated with purging that will be discussed later in this chapter. Second, purging helps legitimize bingeing; that is, by undoing the binge, purging makes bingeing more likely to occur in the future.

The range of behaviors may vary greatly from person to person. While some of our patients binge and purge several times daily, some binge and purge only on occasion. What different individuals consider a binge is also variable. For one person, a binge might be five thousand calories of sweet foods, while for another a binge might be eating any food that is not low in calories. Likewise, purging can take several forms. Although most bulimics induce vomiting, some seldom or never vomit. Others may combine methods of purgation, such as vomiting and laxative abuse or fasting, excessive exercise, and diuretic abuse.

## How is Bulimia Different from Other Eating Problems?

The three most common eating problems are anorexia nervosa, bulimia, and compulsive overeating. Bulimia is both similar to and different from the others. Although it appears to the lay person that it is more similar to compulsive overeating, it is actually more like anorexia. The similarities between anorexia and bulimia include a preoccupation with dieting, food, weight, and body size; a discomfort when eating with others; and approval seeking. Also, many bulimics have previously been anorexic, and many of those who have not been anorexic wish that they could be, that is, be able not to eat.

As similar as anorexia and bulimia are, they also differ in several ways. One difference involves denial of the problem; the anorexic denies to others and to herself that any problem or abnormal eating behavior exists, whereas the bulimic usually denies the existence of a problem to others but clearly recognizes that her eating is abnormal. Also, the anorexic is always underweight (at least 15 percent below recommended body weight), but the bulimic can be underweight, normal weight, or overweight. Although the anorexic and the bulimic both exhibit *body-image distortion* (the body is misperceived as being larger than it actually is), the distortion of the anorexic is typically more severe than that of the bulimic. Finally, the anorexic's goal is to lose more weight, but the bulimic's goal is to attain an ideal, often unrealistic weight or shape.

Other abnormal eating problems (e.g. compulsive overeating) are in fact *problems* for many individuals, but are not considered to be eating *disorders* as classified in professional diagnostic manuals. Likewise, obesity is not considered a psychiatric disorder but rather a physical disorder. The bulimic will overeat at times, as will the compulsive overeater. However, the dynamics involved, and often the personalities of the individuals, tend to be different. As a result, treatments effective for compulsive overeaters tend not to be helpful for the bulimic.

A discussion of eating problems would not be complete without a comparison to normal eating. Obviously, each of these eating problems differs from normal eating. It should be pointed out, however, that normal eating is not "perfect" eating. Most people make mistakes with their eating. That is, they may sometimes eat too much, too little, or foods that are not particularly nutritious. They may diet reasonably for short periods, or they may make changes in their eating habits in an effort to set up healthier eating regimens.

The primary difference between normal eaters and bulimics has to do with the intensity of the bulimic's emotional responses prior to, during, and following eating. That is, normal eaters typically do not feel overly anxious, afraid, guilty, or out of control with regard to eating. Additional differences include the frequency and intensity of eating mistakes. More specifically, most normal eaters do not usually overeat on a regular basis nor ingest the large quantities of food that are often characteristic of the bulimic's binges. Finally, most normal eaters do not purge regularly. They may compensate for overeating by restricting food intake or increasing exercise. Some may occasionally take a laxative or diuretic because they feel constipated or bloated from overeating. Few induce vomiting. Most normal eaters are simply able to live with their eating mistakes without feeling compelled to undo them.

## Isn't Bulimia a Lot Like Alcoholism or Drug Addiction?

Yes and no. It is like alcoholism and drug addiction in that a substance is being put into the body in an effort to indirectly deal with one's life problems. It is similar in that it may worsen as depression worsens and that it also causes depression; it is similar in that it creates both physical and psychological problems; and it is similar in that it becomes more of a problem over time and is difficult if not impossible to get over without professional assistance.

Bulimia is also quite different from alcoholism and drug abuse. It is *not* an addiction. Alcoholics and some drug addicts do not get over their disorder even though they recover and do not use alcohol or other drugs. People often think of alcoholism in terms of "once an alcoholic, always an alcoholic." This is not the case for bulimia. Recent treatment research and our own clinical experience indicate that bulimics do get well. Bulimia is also different in that the alcoholic can live without alcohol and the addict can live without drugs; the bulimic cannot live without food.

Finally, some bulimics do have drug and alcohol problems. The same depression that fuels their eating disorder can lead to alcohol and drug abuse. The same difficulty with impulse control that helps develop and maintain bulimia also makes it easy to experiment with and abuse drugs and alcohol.

If the bulimic is abusing drugs or alcohol, this problem must be managed *before* dealing with the eating disorder. Treating the substance-abusing bulimic will be discussed in greater detail in chapter 8.

## How Can I Understand Bulimia?

Bulimia has three components: the actual eating and purging behaviors, or the *behavioral component;* the way bulimic individuals think about themselves and their world, or the *cognitive component;* and the way bulimics handle their emotions, or the *emotional component*. Understanding bulimia requires understanding all three parts of the problem.

Perhaps the case of Allison can facilitate the understanding of bulimia through identifying the role each of these components played in her disorder. Allison was unhappy and depressed (emotional) much of the time. She believed (cognitive) that her unhappiness was due to her weight and that the solution to her problem was to be thinner. Consequently, she began to diet (behavioral). Unfortunately, she was unable to diet reasonably and became increasingly restrictive with her dieting and more excessive with her exercise (behavioral). Her unreasonable dieting and exercise led to binge-eating (behavioral), which helped her think that she was "bad," had "no will power," and was "out of control" (cognitive). These negative thoughts in turn helped her feel more depressed and lowered her already low self-esteem (emotional). She also felt guilty and afraid (emotional) when she binged, so she felt she had to purge the food (behavioral). As her bingeing and purging increased over time, she felt even worse about herself (emotional), and so the cycle of bulimia went on until Allison entered treatment.

The most important step in understanding bulimia is realizing that bingeing and purging are used to manage uncomfortable emotions. Each of us knows from our own experience that if we feel bad enough, we will do almost anything to feel better. In this regard, bulimics have found that bingeing and purging can temporarily distract them from how bad they feel. Unfortunately, because bingeing and purging are only distractions, these feelings will inevitably re-emerge, necessitating further bingeing and purging.

## How Many People Suffer from Bulimia?

Estimates vary, and accurate figures are difficult to obtain for a variety of reasons. It appears that the prevalence of bulimia among adolescent girls and young women is approximately 1–3 percent, while the prevalence in males is approximately one-tenth of that in females (APA, 1994).

## Are Certain Groups or Types of People More Likely to Develop Bulimia?

Yes. Any group that requires a low body weight or thin shape puts its members at higher risk. This includes dancers and models (Garner and Garfinkel, 1980) as well as some athletes (Thompson and Sherman, 1993). Additionally, sexually abused individuals appear to be at increased risk.

## Why Do People Develop Bulimia?
### WHERE DOES IT COME FROM?
### HOW DOES IT START?

Bulimia almost always begins with a diet or at least with a desire to lose weight. The individual has usually tried every weight-loss regimen available and feels desperate to lose weight. She believes that if she could only lose weight she would be happier and would be able to accomplish much more in her life. Sometimes she accidentally discovers bingeing and purging; that is, she may vomit spontaneously after eating. Or she may hear about "this great way to eat all you want and still lose weight" from a friend. Or she may learn of bingeing and purging via television or the print media. Ironically, many bulimics report learning of purging through television programs and magazine articles designed to inform and warn the public about the dangers of bulimia.

Regardless of where the idea comes from, most bulimic individuals do not intend to use bingeing and purging on a regular basis; they believe they can control these behaviors. Unfortunately, the individuals who are willing to try bingeing and purging are usually the ones least able to control these behaviors. With each binge episode, the behaviors become strengthened through practice and reinforcement. That is, every time the person binges and purges, those behaviors are "stamped in" and become more probable responses to future situations. Additionally, bingeing and purging generally help the person feel better temporarily by reducing her anxiety and fear. This tension-reducing aspect of bulimia also tends to increase its probability of recurrence. Finally, these behaviors become easier for the individual to rationalize; that is, justifying these behaviors becomes easier. Initially, bulimia was to be a seldom-used experiment to assist in weight management. However, through practice, tension reduction, and rationalization, it soon becomes a frequently used compulsion that is out of the individual's control. A thorough explanation of the entire process is presented in chapter 5.

Bulimia is related to familial, societal, and psychological fac-

tors. Additionally, factors more biological in nature, such as a
predisposition to depression, may also play a role. Individual
chapters in this book will address each of these factors, but suffice
it to say at this point that familial, societal, and biological factors
set the stage for the development of bulimia; psychological, or
more specifically personality, characteristics of the individual
provide the determining factor once the stage has been set.

A final note on what bulimia is and where it comes from
involves the issue of control. Bulimics are typically individuals
who do not feel in control of their eating, their feelings, or their
lives. In many ways bulimia contributes to these out-of-control
feelings, but bulimia is also used as a way to manage feelings and
restore a sense of control.

Throughout this book, we will be discussing different aspects
of the relationship between bulimia and control. For example,
when bulimics feel out of control, they are apt to binge and
purge. Through bingeing and purging, they may temporarily feel
the restoration of a sense of control. That is, they are often feeling very tense and anxious prior to bingeing and purging. The act
of bingeing and purging can release some of that tension, thereby
helping them feel more relaxed and in control. Ironically, bingeing and purging may cause them to feel more out of control; yet
in another way, the predictability (certainty) of bingeing and
purging may help them feel in control — at least, they know what
to expect.

The issue of control is quite complex and often paradoxical,
sometimes to the point that it may appear contradictory. Its
understanding is, nonetheless, critical if you are to truly understand bulimia and how it feels and is used by your bulimic friend
or family member. By the end of this book you should have a better understanding of this difficult and complex issue.

## What Are Some of the Psychological Difficulties of the Bulimic?

### INTENSE PREOCCUPATION WITH FOOD

Many bulimics report that they spend up to 95 percent of their
waking hours thinking about what to eat, when to eat, where to
eat, how to binge without getting caught, where to vomit, when

to vomit, how and if they want to use diuretics, laxatives, or diet pills, when to exercise, and when to fast or diet. This preoccupation with food and eating-related behaviors is usually a result of dieting. By dieting, the bulimic makes food and eating more important. More specifically, the more she deprives herself of food, the greater becomes the drive both physiologically and psychologically to binge-eat.

### RELENTLESS PURSUIT OF AN IDEAL WEIGHT AND SHAPE

Unfortunately, the bulimic very narrowly defines "ideal" as thin and perfect. She is convinced that she can be happy only if she is thin enough to achieve the perfect shape. This already illusory pursuit is further complicated by the fact that she cannot get thin (perfect) "enough." Furthermore, this focus on an unrealistic body shape keeps her from getting on with her life (e.g., looking for a job, dating, making friends).

### LOW SENSE OF SELF-WORTH

Common among bulimics is a general sense of low self-esteem. The bulimic sees little that she is good at and then devalues the few skills, abilities, or aptitudes that she is willing to admit to. Positive attributes or outcomes are attributed to luck or some other external force. Low self-esteem contributes to bulimia, which, in turn, further confirms the bulimic's low sense of self-worth.

### LOW SENSE OF SELF-CONTROL

One problem most bulimics suffer from is what we refer to as a lack of impulse control. That is, it is difficult for them to control their impulses or urges. In part, this poor impulse control is due to a low tolerance for frustration and anxiety. Bingeing is simply one more impulse that they have difficulty controlling.

### DEPRESSION, ANGER, AND ANXIETY

There are many feelings, both hidden and overt, that the bulimic may be experiencing. Generally, depression is the most common, but it may be anger, anxiety, or other troublesome feelings, or any combination of feelings. Chapter 7 will discuss specifically how the bulimic deals with feelings and more appropriate and healthier ways she can learn in treatment to manage those feelings.

### ABSOLUTE THINKING

Absolute thinking is sometimes referred to as all-or-nothing thinking or black-or-white thinking. It refers to the way in which the bulimic conceptualizes her world. She sees behaviors, events, and circumstances as all good or all bad; most importantly, she sees herself as fat or skinny — usually fat. There is no in-between for the bulimic. This problem with her thinking will be addressed more fully in chapter 6.

### DIFFICULTY EXPRESSING EMOTION IN A DIRECT MANNER

Most bulimics have never learned how to express emotion directly. Additionally, many fear their emotions may get out of control or displease significant people in their lives. Bulimics use eating as a means to distract (protect) themselves from their feelings. This aspect of bulimia will be discussed in chapter 7.

### UNUSUAL EATING HABITS AND BEHAVIORS

Bingeing and vomiting are, of course, unusual eating-related behaviors. But the bulimic may have many other unusual eating habits as well. The time of day she eats, the way she prepares food (or doesn't prepare food), and whom she will eat with or not eat with may all have an unusual quality to them. Everything may have to be eaten "plain" (no topping). Or she may eliminate entire food groups, such as meat or dairy products.

Although many nonbulimic individuals have one or more of the above eight difficulties to deal with, the bulimic individual has most, if not all, of them with which to contend. One way to think about these psychological difficulties is to consider them as risk factors. Therefore, the more of these psychological problems one has, the greater the risk for developing bulimia.

# Are There Medical Problems or
# Side-Effects of Bulimia?

There are several medical problems that can result from bulimia. We therefore urge all individuals with an eating disorder to consult with a physician. The most common medical problems include:

✓ **An irregular menstrual cycle.** While menstrual irregularities or even loss of the menstrual cycle (amenorrhea) occur more often when the individual is underweight, similar problems occur even with normal-weight bulimic individuals.

**Stomach and intestinal problems.** This can include pain caused by the physical trauma of vomiting, spasms from laxative abuse, or extreme expansion of the stomach from large binges. Constipation and diarrhea are also frequent problems.

**Dry skin.** This condition results from dehydration or loss of water from the body due to vomiting, laxative abuse, or diuretic abuse.

**Dental and gum disease, including erosion of tooth enamel and increased cavities.** These problems are caused by the gastric acid in the mouth during self-induced vomiting.

**Electrolyte imbalance.** This is potentially the most serious problem or side-effect. Purging causes a depletion of the electrolytes potassium, chloride, and sodium. These electrolytes are actually electrically charged ions that are necessary for proper functioning of all of the body's major systems. While many problems can result from an electrolyte imbalance, the most serious are heart irregularities and even death.

**Puffiness and swelling (edema).** Swelling is caused by dehydration from purging followed by "rebound" water retention. This swelling is usually worse after purging has *ended.*

**Throat and esophagus complaints.** These problems are also caused by the physical trauma of self-induced vomiting.

**Parotid gland swelling (under jawline).** This swelling, which sometimes resembles the mumps or a chipmunk-type appearance, is caused by vomiting.

With the exception of dental erosion, most of these problems can be corrected and are reversible once bulimic behaviors have ceased. Again, we urge consultation with a physician.

## How Is This Book Organized?

Chapters 2, 3, and 4 will discuss societal, family, and individual factors that contribute to the development of bulimia. They also suggest ways that these causal factors can be overcome or at least managed.

Chapters 5, 6, and 7 will focus on the three components of the problem: the behavioral, the cognitive, and the emotional. These chapters describe each aspect of this problem and suggest ways to overcome bulimia through a three-pronged approach.

Finally, chapter 8 will provide more general suggestions and strategies for helping a daughter, spouse, or friend get into treatment, and chapter 9 will discuss what treatment is apt to be like. The more individuals in the bulimic's life who can understand the problem and provide a positive therapeutic environment, the easier it will be for the individual to recover from bulimia.

## What Can We Do to Help?

1.  Inform yourself about the problem of bulimia. You have taken a good first step by reading this book and any other material you can find about this problem. Bulimia makes very little sense to the outsider who has neither had the problem nor spoken to others who have bulimia.

2.  Provide as much support and encouragement as you can without being intrusive. There is an extremely fine line between support and control. What is often offered as support, caring, and concern by friends and family is unfortunately perceived as control by the bulimic. Bulimia is a control disorder; that

is, the individual does not feel in control of her life and uses bulimia to try to feel more in control. At the same time, the bulimic wants to be independent and often resents controlling attempts by others. With this sensitivity to control, your support is apt to be misperceived as control. You can offer an open hand, but then you must wait until the bulimic approaches you and takes it.

3. Don't try to be the therapist. Know your limitations. You are too emotionally involved to be able to solve the bulimic's problems. Even therapists seek out treatment with other therapists because it is simply too difficult to see one's own situation clearly. Be who and what you are—family member or friend. Just as bulimic people need the kind of assistance only a therapist can provide, they also very much need the kind of assistance only a friend or family member can provide.

4. Realize that it is most likely going to take professional help for your family member or friend to overcome this problem. It is also going to take time to completely resolve the problem. If bulimia was easy to give up, she would have already done so. Try to develop more patience and understanding for her when she binges and purges by realizing that she is making the best adjustment that she can at the present time. Remember that even though you are afraid, angry, frustrated, and depressed, she is more so and probably has been for much longer.

5. Don't be afraid or embarrassed to seek out professional help or support if *you* need it. There is probably nothing more difficult than watching someone you love hurt herself. The helplessness that family and friends feel can be overwhelming. Take care of yourself, too! Many communities offer support groups for friends and family of the bulimic. You may want to avail yourself of this opportunity.

PART

## II

---

# Causes of Bulimia

Eating disorders appear to result from an interaction of influences coming from our society, the family or social unit, and the individual, including personality and biological factors. No one factor alone is usually strong enough to create an eating disorder. But the more factors present, the greater the chance an individual has of developing bulimia.

The importance of understanding what causes bulimia is *not* to blame anyone. No one—not our society, our families, or individuals themselves—want or hope to create bulimia. We believe that understanding where a problem originates can help you become better equipped to change whatever conditions may have existed to help bring about the problem.

Chapter 2 will discuss the role our society plays in the development of bulimia. Chapter 3 will discuss family factors that frequently occur in families with a bulimic individual. Chapter 4 will discuss those individual factors that put someone at risk for developing the disorder. Obviously, not all individuals who live in our society and come from families with problems develop bulimia. These factors may set the stage, but it is the individual who actually determines whether the disorder occurs once the stage is set.

At the end of each chapter, we have provided what we hope will be helpful suggestions regarding how you might be able to assist someone with bulimia. However, changing the factors that may have caused bulimia does not ensure that the problem will automatically disappear. Once bulimia occurs, it begins to serve many functions and almost takes on a life of its own. Also, bulimia becomes a behavioral habit that is strengthened each time it is repeated.

# 2

# The Role of Society

## How Does Our Society Cause Bulimia?

"Cause" is probably too strong a term, but society certainly contributes to bulimia through its pervasive preoccupation with thinness. People in general, and women in particular, are bombarded in the visual and print media with messages that attractiveness, success, and happiness are dependent on being thin. These continual messages help us imbue thinness with too much importance. In fact, recent studies have indicated that thinness is the most important aspect of physical attractiveness for women. While positive attributes are often associated with being thin and attractive, being overweight carries numerous negative connotations, including "lazy," "out of control," "sloppy," and "ugly." Consequently, as thinness gains higher value and being overweight becomes more taboo, our society encourages women to lose weight at all costs.

With the emphasis given to thinness, weight-loss regimens have become increasingly common. And despite the lack of success with diets (the vast majority of diets do not lead to permanent weight loss), dieting continues to be the most popular regimen. A Nielson study conducted in 1979 found that 56 percent of American women between the ages of twenty-four and fifty-four were actively dieting. This percentage is certainly higher at the present time. And dieting is probably even more prevalent among younger women as evidenced by a recent study (Moses, Banilivy, &

Lifshitz, 1989) that found that 72 percent of a sample of high
school girls dieted. An example comes from one of our patients.
Lisa is a high school student who is confronted over and over
again at school with the importance of dieting. All of her friends
are on diets and are constantly talking about their weight and
how much they are losing or not losing. They may talk about
others who are eating and are "fat." They skip lunch. They exercise together. They compare bodies and compete with each other
to see who can be the thinnest in their group or school. They
notice that cheerleaders and other popular girls are typically
some of the thinnest.

Dieting has become so popular that it is now estimated that
more than $33 billion are spent on the weight loss industry each
year (Wolf, 1991). Much of this is being spent at weight-loss centers, the number of which has also significantly increased in recent
years. As a result of this growing interest in dieting, the number
of articles and books devoted to dieting has increased significantly in the past twenty years. Similarly, Garner and colleagues
(1980) found over 70 percent more diet articles in women's magazines from 1969 to 1978 than in the previous ten years. This
trend increased even more dramatically in the 1980s. But we not
only have magazine articles, we have everything from the out-
landish fad diets promoted in supermarket tabloids to diet books
on the best-seller lists. Dieting has become so pervasive and popular that it is becoming the norm. Unfortunately, this dieting
craze has led many individuals to experiment with diets that
not only do not work, but may also be potentially dangerous or
destructive.

Due perhaps to the fact that diets do not work or at least do
not work fast enough, restrictive regimens are frequently being
supplemented with even more extreme measures. A 1984 *Glamour*
magazine survey involving 33,000 participants found that 50 percent of their respondents used diet pills, 18 percent used diuretics, 27 percent were on liquid diets, 18 percent used laxatives,
45 percent fasted, and 15 percent induced vomiting to control
their weight. What are actually being described in this study are
serous bulimic symptoms. That there is a relationship between
dieting and bulimia should be obvious.

Bulimia almost always begins with a diet. Of course, not all dieters become bulimic. Just which of these dieters becomes bulimic is related to the individual factors that will be discussed in chapter 4. Suffice it to say that dieting relates specifically to bulimia in that dieting leads to, or causes, bingeing. There are both psychological and physiological drives to binge-eat when caloric intake is radically restricted. This is, in part, why most diets fail. Dieters, in an effort to lose too much weight too quickly, restrict their eating too stringently. As a consequence, they "break" their diets and may overeat or even binge. They then berate themselves for failing at their diets, when in fact the psychological and physiological drives to binge-eat were too strong to control through willpower.

As a result of the relationship between dieting and bulimia, messages, either implicit or explicit, promoting or glamorizing thinness are apt to increase the risk of bulimia, at least for some groups of women. The visual media play an integral role in this respect. Thinness messages are communicated both in terms of products and the models employed to sell them.

Although there has recently been some movement in the direction of using models with more "normal" sizes and shapes, most of the models we have been shown in the past twenty years have been significantly thinner than the average American woman. In some cases, they have been so thin that they take on a prepubescent, shapeless, and sometimes even anorexic look. This look has been so pervasive and prevalent in modeling and advertising circles in recent years that it is easy to overlook just how thin these models have become. This process has been insidious—that is, it has been occurring out of our awareness. This is evidenced by the fact that at present a very thin, perhaps even anorexic, leg can grace a pantyhose advertisement without drawing too much attention. That same leg would certainly have been much more noticeable fifteen years ago and would have been received much less positively.

Even though the majority of these models are not in any way representative of the typical physically mature woman, they nonetheless become standards by which women evaluate themselves and in most cases cannot live up to. Their lack of representativeness for mature American women is due to several factors. First, they may be part of the "lucky" 5 percent of women who can maintain such a thin shape (due primarily to genetic factors) without resorting to "heroic" methods such as starvation or purgation. Second, they may actually be prepubescent adolescents, that is, girls who have not yet reached puberty. They have yet to have a menstrual cycle and have not developed a mature shape or figure—no breasts, hips, or curves. Third, they are often made to look more "perfect" than they actually are through the use of make-up and photographic techniques such as air brushing and touch-up. And finally, they may be anorexic or bulimic. As a group, models have a significantly higher incidence of eating disorders.

As powerful as thin models and actresses are in delivering their messages, many advertisements for diet, weight, or exercise-related products are just as powerful. Advertisements in these areas have burgeoned in recent years. Ten years ago, ads would not have mentioned anything about calories. Now we have "diet" or "lite" everything. An advertisement that seems to epitomize the ridiculous end of the continuum involves the number of calories in breath mints (one versus ten); the implication is that this insignificant number of calories is somehow very important and should be taken into account when purchasing breath mints. The most disconcerting part of this advertisement is not the message, however. Rather, it is that this ad is running because it *sells.* That is, people are buying the product *and* the *message.* If they were not, advertising agencies would not be using this type of approach.

We also have advertisements that suggest to us that if we eat normally—that is, do not diet—we will become fat. A recent diet soft drink commercial is particularly illustrative. The setting for the commercial is a party. Hors d'oeuvres are available and people are partaking of these. As they do, they become instantly obese. At the same time, a very chic couple spurns the food, drinking the diet drink instead. Of course, this attractive man and woman remain thin and smile at each other as if to say they know the secret to true happiness: dieting rather than eating. The layman might wonder, "Okay, it's a dumb commercial but what's the real harm?" The real harm is that people at high risk for developing an eating disorder think in concrete terms: "If I eat, I will get fat; if I diet (don't eat), I won't get fat." Interestingly, this particular commercial has generated considerable emotion in many of the bulimics we are treating. Initially, it caused many of them to feel uncomfortable. As they progressed through treatment, however, this discomfort has often become anger. They finally become aware of how they are being manipulated. An advertisement that can generate this much negative emotion can certainly be harmful.

If women and female adolescents are being swayed by the thinness-dieting media blitz, what must be happening with younger girls? We must remember that the children of today have grown up during a very strong television generation. Indications are that they too are susceptible to thinness advertising whether it is aimed at older females or directly at them. A recent article in the *Pediatrics* medical journal (Moses et al., 1989) reported that elementary school children view obesity as being worse than being handicapped or disabled. Also, we are finding younger and younger children dieting. We are also encountering younger girls in our clinical practice who are anorexic or bulimic. There are now numerous summer camps for children whose primary focus is weight loss. We have exercise clothes, tapes, and equipment for children. We even have an exercise gym and equipment for Barbie so she can stay in shape. (Surely, you didn't think Barbie could have such perfectly formed breasts, an incredibly small waist, and those long, thin legs without exercising.) Are young girls influenced by the thinness messages they receive? Very definitely, and this realization recently hit very close to home for one of the authors of this book when he overheard his (then) ten-year-old daughter and three of her friends talking about their fat thighs. Keep in mind that we talking about four thin, virtually shapeless prepubescent girls.

A final note on society's role in the development and maintenance of bulimia indirectly involves these little girls who think they are fat when they obviously are not. Apparently, there is something in society's powerful thinness messages that helps girls and women misperceive and dislike how they look. This is evidenced by the fact that studies on body-image perception indicate that many young women see themselves as larger than they actually are (Klesges, 1983). It is further evidenced by the fact that 76 percent of the dieting women in the Nielson study cited earlier were not dieting because they needed to but for cosmetic reasons.

Body-image distortion and body dissatisfaction have particular relevance for the development of eating disorders. Anorexic girls and women are literally starving themselves in part because they see themselves as being "fat" despite being emaciated. Although body-image distortion is usually not as severe in the bulimic, it does occur at least to some degree in many bulimics and, when teamed with significant body dissatisfaction, makes it difficult for the bulimic individual to ever look "good (thin) enough."

## Hasn't Society Always Valued Thinness?

No. The gaunt look has not always been "in." Different cultures and different times have set different standards. As we look back at the nude women portrayed in the art work of the Renaissance painters, we see a full-figured woman (perhaps obese by today's standards) as the ideal of feminine beauty. As recently as the 1950s, we saw women like Jayne Mansfield and Marilyn Monroe as sex goddesses and as having the ideal female form. Those women were significantly larger than the models of today. When Twiggy came into the public's eye in the 1960s, everyone was appalled at how thin she was. Now that same look has become commonplace and desirable. A study by Garner and colleagues (1980) confirms this trend. They reviewed measurements of *Playboy* centerfolds and Miss America pageant contestants and found that these women have become significantly thinner over the past twenty years.

That times have changed with regard to what is viewed by women as being attractive (thin) was clearly demonstrated recently in an eating disorder therapy group that we were leading. *Sports Illustrated*'s celebrated "25th Anniversary Swimsuit Edition" was currently on the magazine stands. This particular issue was a pictorial display of the covers from the magazine's annual swimsuit editions for the past twenty-five years. Many of the young women in the group had seen the magazine and were discussing it. As a copy of the magazine was being passed around, the women had numerous reactions. Their biggest and most unified reaction, however, related to many of the models of the late 1960s and 1970s. Comments included: "She's fat"; "Gross"; "She's got fat thighs"; "Look at her fat stomach"; "She's got a potbelly." These critical remarks were being made about women who at the time were judged to be attractive enough to grace the cover of *Sports Illustrated*'s annual swimsuit editions. It is interesting to note, however, that some of the group participants even regarded the models of more recent years as not being thin enough. While it is clear that the thin, sometimes emaciated look has not always been valued in our culture, it is equally clear that it is currently overvalued.

## How Do We Learn What Is Beautiful?

As we have discussed earlier, from the time we are young we are exposed to images of glamorous women in the print media, on television, and in the movies. The message is subtle but powerful. The attractive women are smiling, look happy, appear successful and content, and so on. Over time the women have changed. The ads of the 1950s present very different women from the ads of the 1980s.

Different cultures view beauty in many ways, but there is some consensus within each culture as to what is beautiful. For many years, Chinese women were viewed as beautiful if they had small feet. In fact, baby girls used to have their feet bound to prevent them from growing. As adults, women continued to bind their feet and most ended up with extremely deformed and painful feet. Although this procedure is no longer practiced, many generations of women endured considerable pain and disfigurement as they aspired to be beautiful.

Women in the Victorian times endured similar self-torture as they forced their bodies into corsets that were made so small that their oxygen was often cut off and they would subsequently faint. In fact, fainting chairs were provided for them because it occurred so frequently. In addition, many women suffered broken ribs as they were squeezed into those corsets that were to make them look beautiful.

One of the more unusual practices related to feminine beauty occurred in the late nineteenth century. At that time, it was fashionable among many English women to wear gold rings through their nipples. To do so, they had holes bored through their nipples and thin golden rings threaded through the holes. It was believed that wearing such rings made the breasts fuller and rounder, and that the rings were a stimulating sight for men when exposed (Louis, 1983).

We do not have to look to previous centuries to find more examples of women enduring physical discomfort in an effort to be more attractive. Even now, many women regularly wear uncomfortable high-heeled shoes to appear taller and, at least in their eyes, more attractive. Most would agree that high-heeled shoes are less comfortable and less safe for one's posture than low-heeled shoes. Yet many women wear them without complaints. Can you imagine a man voluntarily walking around in something as uncomfortable as high-heeled shoes?

How each society determines what is beautiful is still somewhat of a mystery. But it is clear that the message that develops is strong enough and clear enough that many if not most members of that society come to believe it to be true. Interestingly, the message that develops for women is clearer and more specific than the message that develops for men.

Men do not have a specific look that they are supposed to conform to. They are not expected to look like Tom Cruise, Mel Gibson, Arnold Schwarzenegger, or a top model. In fact, most people probably cannot even name a male model. Men are allowed to look many different ways and still be considered attractive. The standards of attractiveness are less restrictive for men. For example, when a man's hair turns gray, he looks "distinguished."

Women live in a different world from their male counterparts. There is a look they are supposed to conform to. Trying to conform to this look is difficult enough, but the woman's plight is further complicated by the fact that the look changes every year or so. The very thin, shapeless look has recently given way to the healthy, thin, muscular look. In many ways that shapeless Twiggy look closely resembles what little girls' bodies look like. Women are still supposed to have a thin waist, hips, and legs but with a more muscular upper body—a look like top model Elle Macpherson. This new body type is closer to the traditional male shape—small hips and thighs but broad shoulders and a strong upper body. Actually, both body types seem to deny or reject the natural feminine body shape (a soft, rounder body with hips and thighs larger in proportion to the upper body). In doing so, is our culture promoting an antifeminine value? The beauty standards are also much more severe and restrictive for women. When a woman's hair turns gray, she looks "old."

The key issue here is not what uncomfortable or unhealthy practice women engage in under the guise of being attractive. Rather, it is their *willingness* to do so. Many seem not to question how prudent a particular behavior is—they simply accept it. Obviously, some are willing to starve themselves, exercise to exhaustion, or induce vomiting or diarrhea in order not to be "fat."

## Why Are So Many Women Willing to Go to Such Drastic Lengths for the Sake of "Beauty"?

There is probably no one answer to this question. It appears in part to be a result of being continually bombarded with messages that beauty—often synonymous with thinness—is what is really important and that women should always try their best to look as good as they can. If we are shown or told something long enough and often enough, we are apt to believe it (even if it is not true).

Their willingness may also reflect a need for some sort of power in what has been and continues to be a man's world. We all need to feel we have some power and control in our lives. Perhaps some women have seen beauty as an indirect way to have a modicum of power in a male-dominated society in which they are afforded very little, if any, real power.

There is also a competitiveness among women that in part may explain their willingness to resort to uncomfortable or potentially harmful means under the guise of being attractive. This competitiveness may be related to the many thinness and beauty messages they receive and the need for power. Competition among women manifests itself in such a way that if a young woman perceives another as being thinner, she feels she must diet and lose weight because she is not thin enough. It is almost as if she cannot be attractive if the other person is thinner. This competitiveness changes the rules about attractiveness; it goes a step further than "you have to be thin to be attractive"; it suggests that only the thinn*est* can be attractive. This is reminiscent of a young woman one author worked with whose goal was to become "the thinnest person." She fortunately did not become the thinnest person, but it was not for lack of trying. She was able to starve herself to the point that she had to be hospitalized after losing consciousness due to malnutrition, dehydration, and neurological abnormalities.

When we ask our patients about this competitiveness, most are not sure what they are competing for. Some say they are not competing, but admit that they like being thinner than others; some admit that they like being able to wear smaller sizes than their friends.

Other patients say they are competing for male attention. However, if men are asked what they like, most will report that they do not like women who are too skinny. It appears that women who use men as their reason for competing are misconstruing men's dislike for fat women. Most women believe that men do not like (date, marry) fat women. This belief may in fact be true for most men. That is, when asked if they like fat women, most men will probably say "no" (although there is a minority of men that report being attracted to obese women).

The key issue here is not what men like or dislike. Rather, the key issue is the adjective "fat." What constitutes "fat" for many women appears to have been affected by society's tremendous emphasis on thinness. In order to make sure that they are not fat, many women feel they need to be overly thin. Of course, they do not see this thinness as being overly thin; they see it as *not being fat*. This mode of thinking and perceiving is facilitated by the eating-disordered woman's absolute thinking; she believes that if she is not (overly) thin, she must be fat—there is no in-between (normal size and shape) for her.

Now let's put the variable of what men like back into the equation. What women consider fat and what men consider fat appear to be quite different. Even younger men in their teens and early twenties—men who have not really known another time when female models, actresses, and other very visible women were more normal in size and shape—do not seem to want women to be as thin as women think they need to be. A recent Gallup survey reported in *American Health* (Britton, 1988) indicated that younger men do have a preference for thinner women. However, the survey also indicated that "although women *think* men like them lean, a full 65 percent of men say the ideal woman has an average body type; only 18 percent think thin is heavenly." More specifically, men said they liked women to have a "full rear," "medium-width hips," "small- to medium-sized waist," and "medium-sized breasts."

Finally, we are unsure where the competitiveness with regard to shape and size originates, but it undoubtedly creates considerable distress for many women. An excellent example is provided by one of our patients, who felt this competitiveness while attending her university's football game. Kim reported that she spent the entire game "watching all of the thin, pretty girls." She remarked that she was unable to watch the game and enjoy herself. In fact, she left the game feeling quite depressed and fat. Ironically, Kim is a very thin and attractive young woman. Somehow, this competitiveness makes it impossible for her to feel good about herself and appreciate her own attractiveness.

## What Effect Has the Women's Movement Had on Women's Ideas about What They Should Look Like and Who They Should Be?

In many ways, society's traditional messages regarding what a woman should look like and what she should be have persisted despite the best efforts of the women's movement. This in large part speaks to the power and pervasiveness of these messages and the visual and print media that communicate them. Unfortunately, it may also speak to the type of person who is at risk for developing bulimia and how that individual receives the important message of the women's movement.

The women's movement rightly and appropriately encourages women to give up traditional roles and aspire to be whatever they want to be. We believe that this is a very healthy message for women, and we use it in treatment. For some women however, it has probably contributed to their confusion and ambivalence regarding their identity (who they are and who they want to be). Most bulimic individuals have difficulty making decisions, especially when trying to do what is "best" or what "should" be done.

This confusion and ambivalence that tend to be characteristic of the bulimic individual can further complicate decision making. As one young woman said, "I don't know what to do. I'm afraid to do what I want rather than what they [my friends] want because they will be mad [and not like me]." They are afraid that if they eat what they want they will "get fat" (gain weight) and will be rejected. Or, as one married patient said, "If I'm assertive and stand up to my husband, he'll probably divorce me."

Unfortunately, the fear and apprehension the bulimic person feels about focusing more on her own needs and desires is not totally irrational or unrealistic. In some instances, the individual's relationships are related to pleasing and being accommodating. That is, others have come to depend on her meeting their needs. Sometimes they depend on her to be "thin and pretty." When she attempts to change and be more attentive to her own needs, others are sometimes angry and rejecting. They may even indicate that she is being "selfish," or make negative comments about her weight gain. In an extreme case, the married woman mentioned previously did become more assertive and stood up to her husband. He did in fact divorce her. More positively, these are the minority of cases. People who really care about the bulimic and her happiness typically respond well to her attempts to take better care of herself.

This process of asserting oneself in terms of what one wants or does not want is quite difficult for the bulimic individual, who often fears rejection because she believes that she is "not good enough." She may try to compensate by being thin and "perfect." She is much more concerned about pleasing (or actually, not displeasing) others than pleasing herself. She often believes that she has little to offer as a person so she must at least "look good." Consequently, she thinks that her relationships and life will be better if she pleases others. We tell our patients that there is nothing wrong with pleasing others, as long as it is not at their own expense.

Even though most of our patients embrace traditional views of women, many of them nonetheless can see that they "should not be so affected by what men think and expect," or more broadly by what society communicates and seems to value. In fact, many become angry with themselves for not being stronger. They feel considerable conflict in this regard. Unfortunately, this conflict and resulting psychological discomfort may worsen an existing disorder.

Some patients respond to their negative emotions in these instances by "bingeing and purging" to deal with the feelings.

Finally this section should not be concluded without a brief expression of our own thoughts and feelings about the women's movement. In short, we are very supportive of "feminism" (political and social equality for women) and the movement in particular. Thus, this section should in no way be construed as an indictment of the movement or its valuable messages. In fact, it is interesting to speculate about the relationship between adopting, understanding, and living from a more "feminist" perspective and the development of eating disorders. We would guess that a woman's risk for developing an eating disorder would decrease as she was able to live her life more from a feminist perspective. For an excellent account of this notion, the reader is directed to Fallon, Katzman, and Wooley (1994).

## How Realistic Is It to Expect Everyone to Be Thin?

It is not realistic at all. According to the Metropolitan Life Insurance (1983) weight tables, the expected weight for women under thirty years of age has actually been increasing during the past twenty-five years. At the same time, women's desired weights have decreased. This means that what women actually weigh and what they would like to weigh are growing further apart. Therefore, the intense pressure on women regarding weight is really pressure to conform to an *unrealistic* standard of feminine beauty. The absurdity of expecting everyone to be thin is like expecting everyone to be the same ideal height. It sounds silly to say that all women should be 5' 7" and that every effort should be made to attain that ideal height. Yet, in many ways, we apply that same mentality to weight, assuming that all women are capable of, and should be, a particular societally determined weight. The pressure to diet has led to more unrealistic dieting goals and more destructive dieting methods.

Each person actually has a *set-point weight*—a weight determined primarily by heredity to be appropriate. Many young women today believe these set points are too high and refuse to accept them. At the same time, the body is geared to maintain this weight and resists attempts by the individual to drop significantly below it. Unfortunately, many young women are willing to resort to "heroic" means (i.e., starvation, purging, excessive exercise) in order to force their weights to suboptimal limits.

## Even Though Our Society Stresses Thinness, Doesn't It Also Focus on Food?

Absolutely. Have you ever noticed how food has become a part of most holidays, family functions, and general socializing? Thanksgiving dinner, Christmas treats, Easter candy, Valentine's chocolate, and Halloween candy are just a few examples of how holidays in our society have become associated more with food than any other single tradition. Most family reunions or special times together also revolve around food. Even general social activities — office parties, neighborhood picnics, school activities, and the like — have food as a major focus. On the one hand, it is sometimes impolite to reject food when it is offered. On the other hand, we are expected to watch our weight. This double message contributes to a pattern that helps promote bulimia. In no place is this double message more apparent than in women's magazines. Not only do these magazines provide continual information on dieting, they also regularly provide recipes for "irresistible, scrumptious desserts."

For some families, socializing occurs solely around eating. In fact, mealtime may be the only time some families see each other. One of our patients complained that her family never did anything together except eat. This same person also noted that her family placed considerable importance on appearance and thinness. Another patient, Mary, made a similar observation. As a college student, she is often confronted with the bind to eat and not eat when she returns home for a visit. Her mother, in an attempt to be helpful and be a "good mother," prepares all of Mary's favorite foods — many of which Mary is afraid to eat for fear of bingeing or weight gain. Mary wants to please her mother so she will eat when she does not want to and will not say anything to her mother about food selection or preparation for fear of displeasing her. At the same time, she may be secretly angry with her mother for preparing these foods and encouraging her to eat them.

# If We All Grow Up in the Same Cultural Society, Why Are There So Many More Women than Men with Bulimia?

As discussed earlier, our culture's message on thinness is aimed at women rather than men, and men do not have an established look to maintain. Additionally, it is more acceptable for men to be overweight. In fact, small men are often looked down on in our society. Somehow, women are expected to be thin and are sometimes discriminated against if they are overweight.

Interestingly, the emphasis on thinness has become more and more focused in the male direction. As a result, there are many more men dieting now, and the number of men jogging and exercising is increasing. Apparently, many men are using these mechanisms to help them deal with their emotional lives as we are seeing them become compulsive (obligatory or ritualistic) about diet and exercise. That is, they feel guilty about breaking their diets and feel the need to compensate for this through fasting or excessive exercise. Or if unable to exercise for some reason, they may feel guilty, depressed, or anxious. Like many women, some men are using dieting, weight, and exercise as distractions from their real difficulties. Also, like many women, some men are actually competing with other men now in an effort to be thinner than their exercise buddies. If these trends continue, we will see more male bulimics in the future.

Recent research suggests that between the ages of thirteen and thirty, one in approximately four hundred men has an eating disorder. As with women, certain subgroups of men appear more at risk, including wrestlers, models, long distance runners, dancers, and gay men.

Unfortunately, very few men seek treatment. Societal pressures make it more difficult for men to seek treatment, regardless of the psychological problem. They are expected to be stronger and better able to handle their own difficulties. While admitting to an eating disorder is difficult for women due to their need to be perfect, it is even more difficult for men. Not only are they admitting to a problem, they are admitting to one that has been labeled a woman's problem.

# Will Society Ever Change Its Standards for Beauty (Thinness)?

Fortunately, minor movements in a more realistic direction are already occurring. We are beginning to see a few more advertisements using models who are at least not bone thin. This is not to say these models are average-sized women; they are not. They are still thinner, but again the movement is in the right direction. Additionally, a recent poll (Britton, 1988) that surveyed the actual and ideal body shapes of the average American suggests movement away from a bony thin to a muscular thin for women. While this is probably positive, there is still a considerable disparity for women between how they look and how they would like to look. According to the survey, the average American woman is 5' 3" tall and weighs 134 pounds but aspires to be an inch taller and 11 pounds lighter. Unfortunately for many of these women, the probability of them being able to lose 11 pounds and keep it off is about the same as them growing an inch. For this reason, some of these women (depending on individual factors) will be at risk for developing an eating disorder.

# What Can We, as Family Members and Friends of the Bulimic, Do?

1. Let your bulimic family member or friend know that her size and shape are not of primary importance to you. Communicate that you care about her and her happiness rather than what she looks like. Let her know that you love her for who she is, not for what her weight is. As you focus more on her inner qualities and less on her exterior appearance, you will be sending a valuable message as to what is really important to you.

2. Challenge societal values. Do not simply buy into what society tells you about weight and body shape. Bulimic individuals have more difficulty opposing societal values when their parents, siblings, friends, or spouses value thinness. When you observe messages that portray thinness as a worthwhile goal,

let your bulimic friend or family member know that you dis-agree with today's values and emphasis on weight and body shape. This will require a good, hard look at your own values regarding weight, diet, and attractiveness.

3. Work on your own awareness of the subtle and sometimes insidious influence that the visual and print media are push-ing at us; that is, carefully examine the models and the infor-mation that we are presented through advertising. Unfortu-nately, this is sometimes easier said than done. All of us are influenced by our society, and it will take persistent efforts to counter what is so readily accepted by others.

4. Write to magazines and sponsors of products that promote a thin image and let them know of your disapproval. "Thin" sells, and until we stop buying those products, sponsors will continue to promote the very values that promote bulimia. We are aware of one candy company that discontinued its campaign theme of "you can never be too rich or too thin" as a result of complaints to the company. One mother wrote in saying, "You *can* be too thin . . . it is called anorexia and it kills." Business and industry will respond, but it takes an enor-mous effort on the consumer's part to inform them of your concerns.

5. If your daughter, sister, or friend believes she must stay thin at all costs for a particular boyfriend or man, suggest to her that she talk to him. Encourage her to find out what he really wants and why. As discussed earlier, most men do not even prefer the very thin body type. If what he wants is reasonable and she shares a similar goal and desire, then it is acceptable for her to make healthy efforts to comply. But if what he wants is unreasonable or she does not want to comply, she should be encouraged to pursue her own preferences. If she realizes what he wants is purely cosmetic and superficial, she should be urged to seriously consider how the relationship can be re-established on more important issues or whether the rela-tionship should continue at all.

# 3

# The Role of the Family

T HE family is usually the most influential unit in an individual's life. "Family" may refer to parents, grandparents, siblings, spouse, or even to in-laws. Or it may refer to any other person or group most important to an individual. When we refer to family, we are referring to those people who have had the most influence, either past or present, in the bulimic person's life.

## How Is the Family Involved?

The family can contribute to the development of bulimia by providing the environment, values, attitudes, and behaviors that are modeled and reinforced within that unit. Of course, no family intends to make a family member bulimic. In the hundreds of families we have worked with, we have yet to see one family that wanted to create or intentionally encourage a family member to become bulimic. Nevertheless, certain families are more likely to produce bulimic children than are other families, and bulimia is "needed" by these families. When we use the term "need" in this context, we mean that bulimia serves one or more purposes or is needed in some way by the family in order to function. These purposes and needs will be discussed in a later section of this chapter.

# What Family Factors Increase the Risk of Bulimia?

One common factor found in most families with a bulimic individual is poor or destructive communication. These families rarely model or encourage direct and open emotional expression because the parents never learned from their own parents (who never learned from their parents, and so on) how to express feelings in a comfortable and appropriate way. Therefore, the children in these families grow up in an environment in which there are few, if any, healthy outlets for emotional expression. As these feelings and frustrations build up, the bulimic family member turns to food as a distraction from dealing with upsetting feelings. The parents may have dealt with their feelings by obsessing and relying on cognitive means. Although this style may appear to work for the parents, it is maladaptive for the bulimic.

Alcohol problems are also common in bulimic families. Of course, if the family system does not allow for direct emotional expression, an indirect one must be found. The bulimic family member is using food while other family members may be using alcohol. The alcohol use or abuse may also be related to an underlying depression in the parent; that is, the genetic predisposition to be depressed may have been passed on to the bulimic family member. Alcohol abuse, like bingeing, also implies a lack of impulse control (difficulty resisting the urge to engage in potentially harmful behavior). Therefore, families in which feelings, especially depression, are dealt with indirectly, and in which there is a lack of impulse control, are more likely to produce bulimic children. Obviously, families that contain an alcohol problem would certainly qualify in this respect.

Most bulimic families emphasize diet, food, weight, or physical attractiveness. Parents may diet frequently or comment on their own body size or the shape of others. Likewise, there may be certain injunctions or rules about eating, such as "Clean your plate," "Don't waste food because there are starving children in India, China, Ethiopia," and so on. Families that place such a strong emphasis on food, diet, and body size are obviously communicating to children the importance they place on food, eating, and weight. One patient told us about her family's tradition of "starvation corner." Dinners in her family were served "family style" in which a plate of food began at the head of the table and was then passed around to everyone. Whoever was heaviest had to sit in "starvation corner," which was the last seat to receive the food. And at times, there was not much food left. This tradition was intended to be an incentive or way to help family members lose weight — but one that gave a powerful negative message!

Finally, the family may have perpetuated the "good girl syndrome." This syndrome was illustrated in our first family meeting with Connie and her parents. Connie, a sixteen-year-old cheerleader, was described by her mother as "a perfect daughter." Connie was noticeably uncomfortable with this description and became more uncomfortable as her mother continued. "We've not had an ounce of trouble with Connie until this eating problem. She has always done exactly what we wanted her to do. And we are very proud of her." Connie had learned very early that "being a good girl" meant pleasing mom and dad and that the best way to do this was to do what they wanted her to do.

This "good girl" system that operated in Connie's family provided considerable pressure to be bulimic. She felt she needed to be perfect so as not to displease her parents. In order to do this, however, she had to put her own needs on hold, which left her feeling frustrated and depressed. But Connie could not express her frustration and depression, again for fear of displeasing her parents. Bulimia provided her an indirect outlet for these feelings.

When discussing the factors that help provide an environment for the development of bulimia, many families have a tendency to feel guilty. Our intention is *not* to blame anyone. Obviously, no one intends for someone they care about to become bulimic. But important family issues must not be ignored. The family is such a powerful agent for the bulimic. Family members need to understand their roles in maintaining the bulimia, as well as how it serves one or more purposes in their family. Through this understanding, the family can then use its power to facilitate positive change. Family issues are extremely complex and multifaceted. In a closed system like a family, everyone affects everyone else. While the family may affect the bulimic individual, the bulimic also has an enormous impact on

the family. Usually, the impact bulimia has on the family is
related to its purposes in the family.

## What Purposes Can Bulimia Serve in the Family?

Although bulimia may serve a different purpose in each family,
there are some commonalities that exist. For example, it can help
distract family members from another "real" problem, such as
when bulimia is used to protect a bad marriage. That is, it can
keep the focus on the bulimic's eating rather than on a troubled
marital relationship. In that bulimia serves distracting and protective purposes in the family, family members may unknowingly
support or encourage it. This is not to say that they want a
bulimic family member, but they may need one. As long as the
bulimic individual has this problem, the focus is apt to be on her.
Often we find that as the bulimic improves, other family members
unknowingly interfere with recovery. Frequently, the bulimic gets
well before the family. Because the family is intimately tied up in
creating, maintaining, and exacerbating the problem, it is important that the family play a role in treatment.

A vivid example of this phenomenon occurred within Paula's
family. Paula was a seventeen-year-old high school student who
lived at home with her parents. Although her parents had had
marital difficulties for years, the problems had intensified recently, and Paula had become both more aware of these problems and
more uncomfortable with them. In an attempt to manage her discomfort and uneasiness about the possibility of her parents
divorcing, she began to binge and purge. At first, the bulimia was
used simply to distract herself from her uncomfortable feelings,
but then she discovered that the bulimia also distracted her parents from their own difficulties. That is, her parents now had to
unite to handle Paula's problem and, in doing so, were able to
avoid dealing with their marital problems.

A second function of bulimia is that it might help a family
member get the attention that she needs. This is not to say that
she binges and purges simply for attention. She is really asking
if someone will attend to her. Bingeing and purging eventually do

get someone's attention; perhaps it is an emotionally distant parent whom she is trying to reach. In actuality, attention is not enough. She needs to be attended to emotionally in order to feel the acceptance, approval, and love that she desperately needs. More specifically, she wants someone to notice her feelings and to ask how she feels; she wants someone to really listen to her, to accept her feelings, and to try to understand how she feels; and finally, she wants someone to respond to *her*—not to what she does or does not do but to *her* and *how she feels*.

The case of Gail provides an illustrative example. Gail loved her father deeply and very much needed him to attend to her. Due to his work demands, however, he seemed to have very little time for her. This was confusing for Gail because he had spent much more time with her when she was younger. Now that she was older, he was less and less available. He also seemed less comfortable talking with her about personal issues and less comfortable showing his affection. Unfortunately, Gail interpreted these changes as being indicative of his disapproval of her. Her bulimia became one more potential source of disapproval. Consequently, she felt she had to keep it from him. Yet, she admittedly hoped he would notice that she was having problems and demonstrate his caring and concern. Her bulimia was not so much an attempt to obtain attention as it was an attempt to get him to attend to the emotional part of her. Gail needed her father to notice that she was not feeling well and to ask how she was feeling. The importance of this type of responding should not be underestimated. Many of our patients tell us how pleased they are when the significant other person (i.e., parent, spouse, friend, coach, etc.) finally responds in this way. This appears to many of our patients as a breakthrough in their treatment but, more importantly, it simply feels good to them.

Another purpose of bulimia might be to express power and control. The bulimic often feels powerless and not in control of her life. Her bingeing and purging can be sources of power and control in that no one can control these or take them away. Her need for control in large part occurs because she generally responds to the needs of others rather than to her own. Or she may feel controlled and smothered by a confining relationship with a parent. Through bulimia, she has found something that no one can control or take away; that is, no one can stop her from bingeing and purging. She may for the first time feel powerful, although it is a form of power that is usually unhelpful, if not harmful.

A good example of bulimia being used as a source of power and control with a controlling parent comes from the case of Becky. Becky grew up in a family in which most of her decisions were made by her mother. Not only did her mother choose her friends and the clothes she wore, but Becky's mother also determined what everyone was to eat. Mother served dinner, and Becky was expected to eat what her mother served—no more and no less. Mother also had a habit of reading Becky's diary and notes from her friends. While her mother's behaviors were motivated by her concern for her daughter's welfare, Becky felt controlled and felt a lack of trust. She needed something of her own that her mother could not control or take away. Becky's bingeing and purging usually followed inappropriate attempts by her mother to control her. As much control as her mother had in most areas of her daughter's life, there was one area—her bingeing and purging—that she simply had no power over. For this reason, Becky very much needed to hold onto her bulimia, at least until she could find or develop other sources of power and control.

Finally, bulimia may help the family handle separation, individuation, and attachment issues. As a child grows up and approaches adolescence, a need for autonomy and independence emerges. This usually begins at about age fourteen, which not coincidentally is also the time that many eating disorders begin to develop. During this period, the adolescent needs to become more independent and develop relationships outside the family. For a variety of reasons, the bulimic individual often has difficulty with this transition. She feels her need for autonomy and, therefore, may feel smothered by her mother or father and need to separate. At the same time, her emotional immaturity makes separation a fearful proposition. On the one hand, she needs to break away; on the other hand, she is afraid to sever this sometimes stifling tie with the family. Parents of bulimics often unknowingly make this transition even more difficult. They may be overprotective and need to hold onto their daughter; they may discourage or prohibit relationships outside the family; they may make her choose between "them" and "us"; they may show anger, hurt, or disappointment at her attempts to separate. Consequently, the anxiety and fear the bulimic adolescent already feels regarding separation are now exacerbated by her fear of displeasing her parents.

When needs for autonomy are thwarted, the individual can become frustrated, angry, and depressed. The eating disorder may serve as a means for dealing with these feelings. Unfortunately, however, bulimic symptoms often help the family legitimize its need to control the bulimic family member. The bingeing and purging may be used to deal with the family's control, but they only help the family believe she cannot be in control of her life. Although the disorder may develop in the early teens, it is apt to persist until a healthy separation finally occurs.

A final note on separation involves the nature of the relationship between the individuated bulimic person and her family. A healthy separation does not mean a relationship or attachment no longer exists between the bulimic and the rest of the family. It simply means the nature of the relationship or attachment has changed. The bulimic individual is no longer a child, but is a growing and developing adult, and she needs to be treated as one.

## Are All Bulimic Families Alike?

Each family is quite different, but enough commonalities exist that Root, Fallon, and Friedrich (1986) were able to describe three common family types. Actually, most families are a combination of these types with their own unique features. The three types described by Root and colleagues are the "perfect family," the "overprotective family," and the "chaotic family."

The perfect family appears successful and the bulimic appears to be the perfect "good girl." This is a family in which appearance and reputation are of utmost importance. Family loyalty is very strong; therefore, family secrets and problems are hidden. There are clear and rigid ideas about family achievement, and members are expected to comply. Family members are expected to keep a happy exterior and always look on the bright side—to the point of avoiding any problematic feeling or situation. Appearance and achievement are most highly valued.

The perfect family is typified by the bulimic individual who, upon entering treatment, describes her family in glowing terms. One young woman described her father as "awesome." Another described her parents as "the best—they couldn't be better." Sometimes the descriptor "perfect" is used. This overly positive evaluation of the family is characteristic of the denial that occurs in the perfect family. This denial prevents family members from being aware of problems within the family or with individual family members.

Very often members of the perfect family are high achievers, which helps the bulimic believe that family members are perfect. Unfortunately, this belief puts even greater pressure on the bulimic to live up to unrealistic expectations. It also makes it easier for her to believe that *she* must be the problem.

The overprotective family lacks a fundamental trust in the ability of other family members, especially the bulimic, to take care of themselves. These families make it particularly difficult for the bulimic to separate because she is taught that no one outside the family can take care of her or can be trusted. This mistrust is communicated by a parent, usually the mother, who has sometimes been a victim of abuse and has never resolved these past issues. Obviously, this type of family system does not encourage children to be autonomous and independent, which precludes their developing a sense of their own competence. This system, nonetheless, works for the overprotective family because the children will not feel confident enough in their own abilities to leave home. The case of Becky discussed in the previous section of this chapter illustrates this family type.

In Becky's case, her bulimia was used to feel more in control in a family situation in which she felt controlled by her mother. It was also probably used by her to release the pent-up emotion engendered in her through the confining and stifling situation she found herself in. Unfortunately, it was also eventually used by her mother to prove Becky's incompetence—that is, her inability to leave home and run her own life.

The chaotic family is what the name implies—unstructured

and unstable. Frequently, the parents are unavailable and the children, for the most part, raise themselves. Alcohol or some other substance abuse is often prevalent. If rules exist, they tend to be inconsistent, and children never know what to expect. The chaotic family is different from other bulimic families in that emotions, especially anger, are expressed more often. Unfortunately, that expression is usually excessive and inappropriate, sometimes to the point of being destructive or violent.

The insecurity and uncertainty of the chaotic family greatly contribute to bulimia in several ways. The case of Diane is illustrative. Her father was absent from the home. Her mother was alcoholic and verbally abusive. Although only sixteen years old, Diane was responsible for her younger siblings. She never knew what to expect when she came home from school each day. Sometimes her mother was drunk and angry, sometimes her mother was not at home and might not return for days. Seldom was there food in the house. There were no mealtimes. Her bulimia served as an outlet for her anger, which was suppressed due to fearing her mother's rage and unpredictable behavior. It also allowed her to escape from her responsibilities of caring for her brother and sister. Bingeing and purging provided the only predictability in her life; bulimia is very predictable—Diane knew what would happen each time she binged. In such a chaotic existence, predictability was the closest thing to security she could find. Bulimia was also a secretive, safe activity that she came to rely on, almost as if it had become her best friend.

## Should the Family Be Involved in Treatment?

Where feasible, it is highly recommended that the family be in treatment. If the family and family environment contribute to the development, maintenance, and exacerbation of bulimia, it makes little sense to treat only the bulimic individual. Without change in the family, the recovering bulimic will likely be encouraged back into the bulimic behavior. In treatment, family members can understand their need for bulimia and can learn how they contribute to the problem. This may be as complex as each family member making significant behavioral, attitudinal, and communicative changes or as simple as learning what not to say, what to say, and when to say it. Family members are obviously powerful people in the bulimic's life. It is important to use that power to be helpful to the bulimic individual. At the least, we want to minimize the family's potentially harmful power. Because the family typically plays such an important role in the problem, we believe it should also play an integral role in the solution.

Another reason for involving the family in treatment is that as the bulimic attempts to change, pressures and difficulties will arise in the family, due in large part to the purpose bulimia serves in the family. Should this occur, these pressures and difficulties can be dealt with directly in treatment.

## Should We Worry about Others in the Family Developing an Eating Disorder?

If the family has produced one eating-disordered individual, it has the potential to produce another. However, this probability is lowered by having susceptible family members in treatment working on family issues and interactional patterns that helped foster the initial eating problem.

## Should Younger Family Members Be Told of the Problem?

Very young children may be too young to understand the problem. For the most part, however, younger members of the family can and should be told of the problem and involved in treatment. Usually, younger family members have a sense that something is wrong in the family. Thus, telling them is not usually an earth-shattering revelation. Additionally, they may feel unfairly excluded if not informed about, or involved in, treatment; and not telling younger children may give the impression that they are part of the problem. We are not only speaking of younger siblings of the bulimic but also the children of a bulimic individual.

# What Can Families Do to Help?

1.  Improving communication is the most helpful change a family can make. The initial step in this process is to let others know you are interested in communicating more effectively with them. By informing them of your interest in this regard, you are already practicing more effective communication by being direct in asking for what you want.

    If you wish to talk with your bulimic family member (or any other family member), be direct in making your wishes known. If possible, try to select a time and setting that will be as convenient and comfortable as possible. Give yourselves adequate time to talk; feeling rushed is apt to impede communication. The fact that you are willing to take whatever time is necessary is itself a positive communication that says the bulimic individual is very important to you.

    When you are talking with her, be sure you are talking *with,* not *at,* her. This is not to be a lecture but rather a conversation. Allow her to say what she needs to say. If you are really listening, you will know when it is time for you to talk. In order to really attend, you will need to focus your total attention on her. This means not doing anything else; put down your newspaper and turn off the TV. It also means that you are not thinking about what you are going to say—you cannot listen to someone else and to yourself at the same time. Additionally, attending requires that you look at her; your eye contact indicates that you are interested and listening.

    Listening is probably the most important aspect of communicating. It implies much more than simply hearing what is being said. If you are really listening, you are not only hearing what she is saying but also what she is *not* saying. Very often the important information is contained in what she is *not* saying; typically, this involves how she is feeling. Feelings are usually more difficult to talk about than thoughts or behaviors. She may be talking about many things that are not really important in an effort to prevent direct emotional expression. Try not to get so caught up in the words that you miss what really needs to be communicated: the feelings.

Notice her body and facial expressions; if they do not seem to fit with her words, she may not really be telling you what she needs or wants you to know. In these circumstances, do not be afraid to ask her how she really feels and what she really wants. A more in-depth discussion of listening to the emotional part of the person can be found in chapter 7.

When it is your turn to talk, be direct and take responsibility for what you are saying by using "I" statements (e.g., "I get upset when you binge and purge"). Probably the best way to be direct is to use as few words, especially qualifiers, as is necessary to convey your message. Directness usually reduces the possibility of communication mistakes by using only words that are necessary. "I" statements make it clear that *you* are expressing *your* thoughts. They also decrease the possibility of making accusatory remarks. Accusations will only make the bulimic defensive and angry, which greatly interferes with effective communication.

Try not to make assumptions about what she is telling you. Test your assumptions by asking for clarification if you are not sure. Untested assumptions are communication errors that significantly interfere with effective communication. Do not be afraid to ask questions; simply try to ask them in a sensitive and caring manner. Harsh questions or accusations frequently feel invasive. Remember that how we say something is often more important than what is being said.

Our discussion of communication to this point has focused on how to talk and listen to the bulimic family member, which presumes a willingness on the bulimic's part to talk. But what if she does not want to talk? You must honor that wish. However, express your continued concern and your desire to talk and to be helpful. Provide reassurance that you will be more than willing to talk with her when she is ready.

2. Work on eliminating the "good girl syndrome." The bulimic feels that the only way to earn the love of others is to please and that to be most pleasing she must be perfect. It is imperative that she knows she is loved for *who she is* and not only for *what she does*. Help her focus more on what *she* needs and wants. Let her know it is okay not to be perfect. Reassure her that it is acceptable to disagree with you and that you are willing to talk out any differences.

3. Be aware that, as the bulimic gets better, other problems are apt to emerge in the family. Remember that bulimia often covers up other family or individual problems. Without the bulimia, the other problems are apt to be more apparent. If these problems are more threatening to the family unit or even more serious than the bulimia, family members may unknowingly pressure the bulimic back into the disorder or try to convince her she has not improved.

   The bulimic individual may be pressured or pushed back into the bulimia through family members reverting back to previous behaviors or interactional styles that fostered the disorder. For example, one patient had used her bulimia to deal with her feelings of powerlessness in the family before recovering. Her recovery was aided by family changes that afforded her more power and control in the family. However, when the "real problem" (bad marriage) surfaced, threatened family members attempted to take the control back.

   When threatened family members try to convince the recovering bulimic that she is not improving, their tactic usually takes the form of criticizing her eating or food choices, often claiming that eating diet foods is a sign that she is not well. It is true that recovering bulimics often continue to eat many of the foods they were eating prior to successful treatment. In actuality, they are usually eating foods not only low in sugar and calories, but also low in sodium, cholesterol, and preservatives—a regimen that is healthy, as long as the quantity and variety of the foods provide the nutrition and calories necessary to maintain a reasonable weight.

   If you are aware that your recovering bulimic family member's eating difficulties have worsened after improvement, talk with her and other family members about who or what might have reverted to a previous unhelpful role or condition. If the unhelpful change can be identified, then work as a family to make the modifications necessary to resume movement in a more positive direction.

4. If other problems in the family do in fact emerge as the bulimic family member improves, try to deal with these as directly as possible. This will probably mean treatment. The bulimia required treatment for recovery; the other problems it masks (alcohol, marital discord, etc.) are also apt to require

treatment for resolution. By seeking or being involved in treatment, you are modeling your willingness to face whatever difficulties may exist in the family. Additionally, talking openly about your fears and concerns regarding treatment would be helpful to you but would also provide healthy modeling for other family members.

5.  Assess the distribution of power in your family. The power structure usually involves decisions and how they are made, as well as rules and how they are enforced. Who has a say in decision making? Does someone have the last say? What are the rules? Who makes them? Who enforces them? These are all questions you and other family members can discuss in an effort to determine your family's distribution of power. Everyone needs a sense of power and control; feeling powerless and out of control can foster bulimia and other problems. If the distribution of power is found to be inequitable, especially if someone is feeling powerless, talk about reasonable ways to modify it.

6.  Just as the bulimic does not have to be perfect, the family does not have to recover perfectly. Try to be patient and tolerant. Most problems in a family have taken years to develop and have been strengthened through years of practice. Consequently, effective change is apt to take some time.

# 4

# Individual Factors

## What Individual Factors Contribute to the Development of Bulimia?

Two individual factors that increase the risk of developing bulimia are personality traits and biological make-up.

## What Is Meant By the Term "Personality"?

"Personality" refers to an organized pattern of behaviors and traits that characterizes how an individual relates to the world. More specifically, one's personality is made up of traits that represent enduring patterns of perceiving, relating to, and thinking about the environment and oneself. Suffice it to say, one normally has a somewhat consistent way of relating to the world, to others, and to oneself. We refer to that pattern as the individual's personality.

There are some people, for example, that we say are "outgoing," while others we describe as "quiet." Without realizing it, most of us categorize or describe people in some way. Maybe they are confident or unsure of themselves, comfortable or uncomfortable in social situations, efficient or scattered, and so on. It is traits like these, along with hundreds more, that make each individual unique. When these traits are taken together they form the personality of an individual.

# What Role Does One's Personality Play in Bulimia?

Because all of us are subjected to societal pressures to be thin, and families generally provide similar environments for all their children, it is the personality that in large part determines who will have an eating disorder and who will not. Parents often marvel at how each of their children is different from the rest. It is usually their personalities that underly their different approaches to life. While our society puts pressure on us to be thin, and families may provide an environment that is consistent with the development of an eating disorder, ultimately it is the individual's response to and handling of that environment which determines whether or not that person will develop bulimia.

Our clinical experience, as well as research findings, indicate some commonalities in the types of people who develop bulimia. That is, the personality patterns of those who have bulimia are more often alike than one would expect might occur by chance alone.

# What Type of Personality Traits or Personality Problems Do Bulimics Tend to Have?

The following traits are frequently found in those individuals who have bulimia. Of course, no one individual has all of these traits, but many of them will undoubtedly sound familiar to you. Also, although we discuss many of these traits as if they are separate entities, we do this only to aid in instruction and understanding. Obviously, these traits overlap and function together in an organized configuration.

### LOW SELF-ESTEEM

Low self-esteem is perhaps the most important trait, both because it occurs so frequently and because it probably does more to maintain bulimia than any other trait. Very simply, low self-esteem means the individual does not like herself. Unfortunately, there is no problem more difficult than changing how a person feels about herself. Although the bulimic person often focuses on her physical self, she actually dislikes her internal self. She is apt to denigrate herself, using a variety of negative characterizations, such as fat, ugly, stupid, worthless, weak, and hopeless.

The person with low self-esteem has a negative system for explaining what happens in her life. If anything goes wrong, she is more than willing to accept the blame because ineptitude and ineffectiveness fit with how she thinks and feels about herself. A good example comes from a patient's sister who was talking about a recent shopping trip she and her sister went on. It seems that another shopper bumped into Cathy (the patient) and Cathy apologized, accepting the blame when she was obviously not at fault.

On the other hand, if something in the individual's life goes right, she is not likely to attribute it to herself because success does not fit with her negative self-concept. When confronted with positive information about herself, the person with low self-esteem is apt to react similarly to a young, single mother we worked with. She did not like herself because she believed she was fat and ugly. Nonetheless, she had a boyfriend who cared for her very much. It was not possible for her to believe that she was not fat and ugly, or that perhaps there were other things about her that attracted her boyfriend. She explained her boyfriend's attraction by saying that he was very insecure and had picked her because he would not have to worry about losing her to another man.

Obviously, with such a negative system for attributing success and failure, the low self-esteem bulimic will find it virtually impossible to change her self-esteem in a positive direction. Her situation is further complicated by the fact that her bulimia and its accompanying depression serve to lower an already low sense of self. As damaging as the physical and psychological symptoms of bulimia are, the most damaging is the negative effect it has on self-esteem.

## NEED FOR APPROVAL/DEPENDENCY

The bulimic individual believes that the truly important things in life that she wants, such as security and happiness, come from others rather than being under her control. For this reason, she is apt to make decisions based on what she believes others want or expect from her in an effort to please them and win their approval. When we describe her as "dependent," we are not referring to the traditional meaning of "dependent." She is not a person who depends on others to do things for her. On the contrary, others are much more apt to depend on her. In fact, her primary role both within and outside the family becomes that of pleaser or caretaker. She is, nonetheless, dependent on others for the temporary and minor sense of esteem she derives from pleasing them. Unfortunately, her need for approval helps her become passive, unassertive, and overly compliant as a result of fearing to displease her only source of good feeling. It also reinforces her belief that she cannot function independently. It affords her no opportunities for developing self-confidence. In order to live like this, the individual must put her own needs on hold, which will inevitably lead to frustration and depression. Regardless of how frustrated and depressed she may become, however, she persists in using this approach to the world because she knows no other way and is afraid to experiment.

Sally, a high school student, provides a classic example of this need for approval. Sally's first priority always seemed to be to please. She was an excellent student and the school environment was an arena in which she frequently applied her need for approval. It was not enough that she make good grades; she also felt a need to please her teachers in other ways. While she was in treatment, she was quite stressed, and one of her major stressors involved an advanced math class in which she was not performing at her usual high level. We finally persuaded her to withdraw from the class. However, when she went to talk with her teacher about withdrawing, she got the sense that he felt he had done something wrong to prompt her withdrawal. In order for him not to feel guilty, Sally changed her decision about withdrawing.

## Low Tolerance for Anxiety and Frustration

Very simply, a low tolerance for anxiety and frustration means that the bulimic has difficulty waiting. In psychological terms, it means she finds it difficult to delay gratification. It is typified by her desire to be thin; she does not just want to be thin — she has to be thin *now!* This impatience with having to be thin in part helps her decide to try desperate and sometimes dangerous means to lose weight. Probably the last regimen she is willing to try is the one that is most apt to work (if any will)—reasonable eating and reasonable exercise—because "it takes too long." If she feels bloated, she must get rid of this feeling immediately through diuretic or laxative abuse. She feels she cannot wait the two to three days of normal eating without purging that would be necessary to deal with this fat feeling. If she feels she has too much food inside of her, her anxiety causes her to feel she must get rid of it immediately. She is too anxious to wait a week to see if the food she has eaten will result in weight gain. The bulimic individual finds it too uncomfortable to sit with her anxiety until it abates. In these situations, she thinks that something awful will happen if she does not take care of it *now.*

Although the previous examples deal with food, eating, and weight, the bulimic deals with other aspects of her life in similar ways. If she expects herself to do something, she expects herself to be able to do it *now.* She also expects herself to be able to do it *perfectly.* These unrealistic expectations relate to virtually all aspects of her life. Although unrealistic expectations create considerable frustration and anxiety in and of themselves, the bulimic individual's plight is further complicated by a belief that she cannot be successful. In essence, she is telling herself she *should* be able to do everything quickly and perfectly while believing she cannot.

It is interesting to note that the bulimic person often attributes these unrealistic expectations to significant others in her life. While it is true that others often do in fact have unrealistic expectations for their bulimic relatives or friends, it is also true that the expectations come as often from the bulimic individual herself. Nonetheless, she worries and is frustrated when she is unable to live up to what she believes are others' expectations. This is, of course, to be anticipated, given her need to please.

Part of the bulimic's difficulty in tolerating frustration is that she feels as though she has been frustrated forever, and to some degree, this is probably true. As has been explained earlier, she has usually put her own needs on hold in order to please others. She lives by the myth that if she does everything right, she will at some point reap her just rewards.

The bulimic's frustration is also promoted by her own deprivation. She often does not allow herself to eat what she wants, when she wants, or how much she wants. She often denies herself simple pleasures because she does not deserve them, in part because she seldom believes that she, or what she does, is good enough.

Part of the bulimic individual's low tolerance for anxiety relates to the fact that she usually already feels anxious for a variety of reasons and thus cannot tolerate more. Her difficulty with anxiety is further complicated by the fact that she attempts to hold back her feelings, which simply creates more anxiety that she must hold back. For these reasons, it is safe to say that the bulimic person is generally quite stressed emotionally. Unfortunately, this engenders more of a need for release and relief through bingeing and purging.

Obviously, the bulimic person's low tolerance for anxiety and frustration can greatly affect treatment. With regard to low frustration tolerance, she expects herself to get well quickly. Unfortunately, bulimia is a very complex disorder that often requires months of treatment in order to get well. Consequently, she becomes frustrated when she does not change rapidly and is apt to want to give up on treatment. This is a time when she very much needs the support and encouragement of family and friends to stay in treatment. With respect to low anxiety tolerance, she will find it difficult to withstand the anxiety necessary for her to get well; more specifically, she will experience considerable anxiety as she attempts to give up dieting or to refrain from purging when she feels she has overeaten. At this point, she may seriously question whether she can get well or even whether she wants to try.

## COMPULSIVENESS

Although this personality trait is more often seen in the anorexic, it is frequently encountered in the bulimic as well. The compulsive bulimic's style can be characterized by perfectionism, orderliness, and rule orientation that often borders on rigidity. This rigid and sometimes impersonal means of relating to the world is designed primarily to deal with her fear and anxiety associated with disapproval. This is evidenced by the rigidity of her schedule.

Taking her eating schedule as an example, she may try to eat the same foods, in the same quantities, at the same time everyday. Anything that interferes with this schedule is apt to frustrate her and make her anxious. She may also have injunctions about eating; that is, she may have to eat all the food she takes; or she may have to always leave food on her plate; she may not permit herself to eat after 8:00 PM; or she may have to eat four bowls of popcorn each night before going to bed. If she breaks a rule or violates an injunction, she is apt to feel guilty and impose even harsher constraints on herself.

The compulsive individual conforms and is overly compliant to the point that she is willing to deny herself what she needs and wants. In fact, it may be difficult for her to even think about what she *wants*. She is a *should* person. That is, her decisions and behavior are guided not by what she wants, but what she *should* want or do. Unfortunately, she becomes so misguided in this mode of thinking and responding that she may even come to value her ability to deprive herself.

The compulsive bulimic's denial and deprivation are not imposed without difficulty, however. In order for her to conform to and comply with rules set down by significant others, she must put her own needs for independence and autonomy on hold. This serves to frustrate, anger, and eventually depress her. Consequently, she is in a bind. She feels she must conform to avoid disapproval, but conforming when she does not really want to angers her. At the same time, she cannot express her anger directly for fear of disapproval. Thus, she is left with expressing her anger through less direct methods, such as bingeing and purging or passive resistance (procrastination, pouting, obstinance, negativity, etc.).

Perhaps our best case example of the compulsive bulimic is Kelly, a college student who will be discussed in more detail in chapter 7. Kelly forced herself to do sixteen hours of academic work daily five days a week. During these times, she allowed nothing to interfere. She denied herself virtually everything (social contact, entertainment, sleep, food, etc.) to stay on her schedule, which was designed to make sure she did not miss anything or make a mistake. As she said, "I have to make sure *everything* is covered."

## IRRESPONSIBILITY

It may seem unusual to talk about the irresponsibility of the bulimic in light of her need for approval, her perfectionism, and her compulsiveness. With such a need to please, to be perfect, and to be orderly and live by rules in an organized manner, how could she also be irresponsible? First of all, most of us are irresponsible about some things, so a small amount of irresponsibility is normal. Many bulimics, however, exhibit what appears to be more than a normal amount of irresponsible behavior.

Regarding her need for approval, many bulimics (and other people as well) live by the myth that, "If I live right and do what I am supposed to do, I will get what I deserve at some point." However, when she is not paid off in what she considers a reasonable period of time, she becomes frustrated and at least for a short time stops trying.

Also, the bulimic's perfectionism and compulsiveness can sometimes lead to what appears to be irresponsibility. Perfectionism often leads to procrastination. She is so afraid of negative evaluation that she will either put off finishing what she is supposed to be doing, citing a variety of excuses, or she will believe that what she is doing is never good enough to be evaluated. To the person trying to understand this irresponsibility, it looks as though the bulimic individual is simply trading one negative evaluation (irresponsible) for the *fear* of another (disapproval). The key word here is "fear." One patient explained it this way: "I can deal with the irresponsibility; it is the fear [of disapproval] that I can't get past."

Some behaviors may also appear to be irresponsible when in fact they are related to fear. For example, the bulimic individual may not show up for a social event she is expected to attend due to being afraid she is too fat or will be expected to eat. She may not keep a therapy appointment because she fears her therapist will be disappointed upon finding out she has been bingeing and purging more rather than less.

Irresponsible behavior may also be a result of poor concentration. The bulimic may lose things or forget to take care of obligations or responsibilities. Often these circumstances are brought on by poor concentration. Her concentration is apt to be poor for several reasons. First, she may be so preoccupied with her eating, weight, and body that she simply does not think about other things. Many of our patients report that they may spend as much as 95 percent of their day thinking about eating and weight-related issues. Second, many bulimics are depressed, and depression almost always impairs concentration. And, third, her poor concentration may be due to the physiological effects of how and what she is eating and how frequently she is purging. The brain needs proper nutrition in order to function effectively; it especially needs complex carbohydrates to aid in concentration. The constant unusual blood sugar levels due to bingeing and fasting, as well as the negative effects of frequent purging, may also decrease concentration.

Finally, some bulimic individuals may also engage in irresponsible behavior as a passive means to being angry. As has been described previously, many bulimics are afraid to show their emotions—especially anger—directly. They nonetheless are often very angry for a variety of reasons. They can more safely express this anger through obstinance, passive resistance, tardiness, holding up others, procrastinating, or a variety of other ways. For example, if she is made to eat, she may hold up dinner by being late, thereby inconveniencing or frustrating family members waiting to eat.

## HISTRIONIC EXPRESSION

The term "histrionic" means lively, dramatic, and even theatrical. The histrionic bulimic seeks attention through the exaggerated expression of emotion. Given that so much of our previous discussion of bulimia has focused on the bulimic not showing her emotions, it may seem inconsistent to now talk about the fact that some bulimic individuals are actually overly emotional. Perhaps a discussion of how the bulimic who dramatizes her emotions differs from the one who denies hers would help clarify this apparent inconsistency. First, and most important, the emotional bulimic is apt to be reared in a family that does not encourage emotional expression, much like her less expressive counterpart. The difference between the two resides in her response to an emotionally discouraging environment. Rather than denying her feelings, she is apt to accentuate and exaggerate her feelings until someone responds to them.

The histrionic bulimic's attention-seeking is quite different from other bulimics in its presentation but is quite similar to others in what she is attempting to accomplish. She is not simply seeking attention, that is, wanting someone to watch or notice her. Rather, she is communicating through her expression that she wants someone to *attend to her*—attend to the *emotional* part of her. She is simply working in a different way to please others in order to receive their approval.

Although the histrionic bulimic is expressing emotion, she is not radically different from the others in that her expression is not what she is really feeling and thus affords her little if any relief. She may be funny, entertaining, or provocative in her presentation while actually feeling much like other bulimics: angry, anxious, afraid, and depressed. Yet like her counterparts, she is not apt to express negative emotion for fear of disapproval. Sheila, for example, typically dressed in an ostentatious, glamorous, and provocative manner. She presented herself in a very happy, engaging, and confident way. She laughed and joked, and everything was always "fine." In actuality, Sheila was quite insecure, felt alone, and seriously questioned whether her mother loved her. Unfortunately, Sheila's presentation or act was not the only thing she did in a big way; she also took fifty to sixty laxatives twice weekly.

Finally, the histrionic bulimic is probably more suggestible than other bulimics. This means she is more easily influenced and swayed by others and what they tell her. For this reason, she is probably going to be even more influenced by society's messages about thinness. She is also probably more inclined to try unusual ways to lose weight.

## DECISION-MAKING DIFFICULTY

One of the primary reasons the bulimic individual has difficulty making decisions is that she has not made enough of her *own* decisions to develop any confidence in decision making. As described previously, the bulimic individual makes her decisions based on what she believes others want. She is usually aware of what she is *expected* to do, but she seldom knows what she *wants* to do. She is afraid that she will make the wrong decision and displease someone. At the same time, she will not be able to please everyone all of the time. Sometimes she becomes so anxious and frustrated in trying to make the right decision that after considerable repetitive deliberation, she will impulsively make a decision simply to "get it over with." Or, she may put off making the decision by distracting herself with bingeing and purging.

The bulimic's difficulty in making decisions may be due not only to the decision itself, but also to what she believes she is supposed to do once the decision is made. More specifically, she is afraid that she will not be able to follow through with the decision — at least not at a satisfactory level. Julie, a young woman who will be discussed in more detail in chapter 7, provides an excellent example. Julie was first afraid to make the decision to leave home for fear of displeasing her parents. Additionally, leaving home meant that she would have to function independently and take care of herself, and she had serious doubts about her ability to do that.

Finally, the bulimic individual has difficulty making decisions due to the lack of certainty in her life. Everything seems like "yes and no" to the bulimic; in fact, her dieting ("No, I don't want to eat"), bingeing ("Yes, I do want to eat"), and purging ("No, I don't") cycle represents a classic example. This uncertainty or ambivalence is in large part a result of the factors discussed in the previous two paragraphs.

## Is It Common for the Bulimic to Lie and Steal?

Some bulimic individuals do lie and steal. This does not make them bad people, however. Nor are they what some people might call pathological liars or thieves. Usually, these behaviors are simply a part of the bulimic-symptom complex; that is, they are consistent with the issues that develop and maintain bulimia. With respect to not telling the truth, the bulimic's lies are often used to avoid disapproval. As we have discussed previously, she has a great need for approval. She has a need to please and, perhaps more important, a need not to displease. She has a need to be perfect and a corresponding need to cover up her imperfection. And, of course, she will have a need to cover up her bulimia in that it is one of the most disliked aspects of herself. In fact, she often refers to her bingeing and purging as a disgusting habit and thinks about how embarrassed she would be if others knew what she was doing. In that lying is so intimately tied to the bulimia, it is probably safe to assume that it will significantly diminish when she is over the bulimia.

Stealing is often much like lying for the bulimic — it is related to her bulimia. Frequently, she steals laxatives or diuretics, either because she is too embarrassed to buy them or because she has to take so many that she can no longer afford them. She may also steal food. Again, the reasons may be that she is embarrassed to buy the food she wants to binge on, afraid that her eating disorder might be detected through her buying, or she is unable to pay for the food. She may also steal money with which to buy food, laxatives, or diuretics; she may feel the likelihood of being found out is less if she does not use her own money, checks, or credit cards. There are also bulimics who may feel that they will be using the stolen money, food, laxatives, or diuretics for engaging in bad behavior, and the bad behavior of stealing seems consistent with this, making it easier to rationalize. Her reasoning might go something like, "I'm already bad and doing bad things. What difference does another bad behavior make?" As with lying, stealing behaviors should significantly decrease or disappear once the individual has gotten over the bulimia.

There is, of course, a much smaller number of bulimic individuals who seem to lie and steal in a manner unrelated to their bulimia; that is, they engage in these behaviors because they find them exciting or because they feel compelled to engage in them. In these cases, the individual may be manifesting a personality disorder that may inhibit or interfere with treatment. In such circumstances, these behaviors may have to be dealt with prior to specific treatment for the bulimia.

## Is It Common for the Bulimic to Be Self-Destructive or Suicidal?

Because the purging aspects of bulimia appear to be so physically destructive, family and friends of the bulimic often assume she intends to harm herself. However, many bulimics are not aware of the potential harm of their disorder. Others deny the seriousness of bulimia. Still others are aware of the potential dangers but have a greater fear of not being bulimic, based on the purposes of the bulimia. Some use signs of physical damage to help them stop bingeing and purging. As one patient said, "When I start vomiting blood, I know it is time to stop."

If the bulimic's intent is to be self-destructive, she is more apt to do it in other ways. This is not to imply that bulimia is never used as self-punishment, however. Several of our patients tell us that they sometimes make themselves binge and purge when they are disgusted with themselves.

A small number of bulimics may exhibit true self-destructive or suicidal behaviors. These behaviors are not typically part of the bulimic-symptom complex. Rather, they are more often the result of a serious personality disorder and its accompanying anger, depression, and impulsivity. In such cases, treatment must focus on these behaviors rather than on the bulimia.

## Most of the Personality Traits Sound Problematic. Are There Also Positive or Helpful Personality Traits of the Bulimic?

Absolutely. The previous list of personality traits should in no way be taken to mean that bulimic individuals are always difficult to be around. On the contrary, they are often some of the nicest, most giving, and most productive people you could ever know. Although they are often irresponsible to themselves and do not take good care of themselves, they try very hard to be very responsible to others and take good care of them. They are typically bright, socially conscious, and hard-working. Many show an innocence and sweetness that is both refreshing and endearing. Many are very social and engaging.

We could go on and on describing the positive characteristics of bulimic individuals because they have many if not most of the positive characteristics we often attribute to people without eating disorders. It is important to remember that people who are bulimic are often not too different from people who are not bulimic. For this reason, as well as many others we will be discussing in later chapters, try not to become too focused on the fact that they are bulimic or, more specifically, on their bulimia-related behaviors. By focusing on their bulimia, you will probably be less helpful to them, and you will also be missing their uniqueness and individuality.

## What is Meant By the Term "Personality Disorder"?

When personality traits like the ones described above are long-standing, inflexible, and maladaptive, and they significantly interfere with everyday functioning, they constitute a personality disorder. Certainly, not all bulimics have personality disorders. But most people with bulimia do have at least tendencies toward one or more personality disorders.

## How Do Personality Disorders Affect Treatment?

Usually these disorders complicate, slow down, or interfere with treatment, thereby lengthening the process. Obviously, the more disordered the personality, the longer treatment generally takes.

## How Changeable Are These Personality Traits?

Personality traits are enduring patterns of thinking, feeling, and behaving. Although they are not the easiest parts of an individual to change, personality traits can be changed if the individual is properly motivated. In most cases, we are not talking about making total, core changes in the person. Usually such extensive changes are unnecessary; these traits do not have to be wiped out in order for the individual to live a fuller, happier life. Rather, we are talking about making more adaptive modifications of these traits. For example, when we assist someone in changing her need to please others, she does not need to eliminate pleasing altogether. Instead, she needs to learn how to please herself and how to please others without it being at her expense.

## What Biological Factors
## Play a Role in Bulimia?

Biological factors that appear to play a role in the development of bulimia are a predisposition to depression and factors related to having a weight and shape that do not conform to the ideal standards promoted by society and embraced by the bulimic. These factors are for the most part due to heredity.

Depression appears to play a significant role in the development and maintenance of bulimia. Consequently, a person who is predisposed to depression is probably more apt to develop bulimia than a person who is not so predisposed. This predisposition is believed to be passed on genetically. However, it may be passed on to some relatives and not others. One daughter may inherit the predisposition while her sister may not. Or, it may not appear in every generation—it might skip a generation. Evidence for this apparent link between depression and bulimia comes from family studies that have found higher levels of affective disorders in the first-degree and second-degree relatives of bulimic individuals than in the relatives of nonbulimic individuals.

The factors related to ideal weight and shape are less clear than those involving depression. First, the individual's body has a set-point weight, a natural weight that the body feels comfortable with and strives to maintain. This set-point weight is primarily determined by heredity and in large part determines how thin an individual can be. If her parents happen to be heavy or even obese, the daughter is apt to have a higher set-point weight than she will be content with. This means that her weight will likely be higher than she will be comfortable with, but it also means that she will find it more difficult to lose weight and be as thin as she would like. Obviously, anything that increases the likelihood of having a higher weight and decreases the likelihood of being able to lose weight and keep it off should increase the probability of developing an eating disorder. More specifically, it seems reasonable to believe that if a woman has a high weight and few if any reasonable and effective means to lower and maintain her weight, she is more apt to resort to "heroic" methods such as bulimia. At the same time, this biological explanation only fits those bulimics who are or have been overweight. Although most bulimics believe they are overweight, many are not overweight and have never been overweight.

The individual's shape will also in part be determined by heredity. If her parents are short, she will most likely not be as tall as she thinks she should be. If her mother has large breasts, hips, and thighs, she is also probably more apt to be larger than she would like in these areas. Thus, these problem areas for her are in large part out of her control. She may, nonetheless, try to force her control on her body through anorexia or bulimia.

## What Can We, as Family and Friends, Do to Help?

There are many ways you might be helpful, some of which we will cover. Before we get into specific suggestions for particular characteristics or problems, however, we want to begin by making more general suggestions to guide your helpful attempts.

In general, you can be most helpful by being as patient and understanding as possible when you see the bulimic displaying her unhelpful traits or characteristics. Often these will be out of her awareness. Even if she is aware, she may not be able to control or change them quickly. Remember, she is probably doing the best she can at the time. If she is unaware, you may be able to help her — awareness is the first step in making a behavior change. Talk with her to determine *how* she would like you to help her increase her awareness. It is usually most helpful to make the person aware at the time that the behavior is occurring. However, given the emotional turmoil that the bulimic is usually experiencing, she may be more receptive to your help after the fact. It may be helpful to you to know that these self-defeating behaviors often occur in response to or in place of an emotion.

1.  Deal with her low self-esteem. As mentioned earlier, low self-esteem is very difficult to change. Probably one strategy that is

not apt to work is trying to convince her that she is better than she thinks she is. This seems especially true regarding compliments on how she looks. As difficult as it is for the bulimic to accept compliments in general, it is even more difficult for her to accept compliments about how she looks. Apart from simply not believing compliments on personal appearance, there tends to be a focus on weight when complimented. A group we were leading for eating disorder patients typifies this. We were focusing on receiving compliments. They reported that if someone told them they looked good, it was taken to mean that they had gained weight. If someone told them they looked healthy, it was also taken to mean they had gained weight. However, if someone said they looked like they had lost weight, they assumed that, because they were still too fat, then they really must have been fat before. If someone didn't compliment them, they assumed they were fat. If someone had complimented them before but not the next time, they assumed they had gained weight. Finally, when this group was asked how they could be complimented and accept it, group members were unable to answer.

Does the bulimic's difficulty in accepting compliments mean she should not be complimented? We believe she should be complimented for several reasons. First, she needs objective and positive feedback to help offset the subjective negative feedback she is constantly giving herself; her feedback works only to strengthen her already negative self-esteem. Second, compliments are a real part of the real world and she needs to learn how to deal with them. And third, as we mentioned earlier, she will assume a lack of compliments to mean that other people view her as unattractive. Although we believe she should be complimented when warranted, we have a suggestion on how to compliment her: sensitively tell her the truth about how she looks, but do it by presenting her with the positive information about herself and simply asking her to think about it and to entertain the notion that she might not be very objective about herself.

You might also try to help her focus on *who she is* rather than *what she does* or *what she looks like*. As has been explained in previous discussions, the bulimic usually grows up in an environment that is achievement-focused, which values her for what she does and rewards her for her accomplishments. In some ways, this is quite normal. For the bulimic, however, it is taken to extremes. Accomplishments and achievements become her *only* source of self-esteem. This is further complicated in that her accomplishments and achievements are never numerous enough nor good enough. Try to focus more on *her*—who she is and how she feels—rather than on her accomplishments or lack thereof. Let her know that what she does and how she looks are fine, but it is *she* that you love and care about.

The bulimic individual not only believes what *she does* is not good enough, she also believes *she* is not good enough. Should you hear her say this or suspect she is thinking it, very gently and sensitively talk with her. Ask her the question, "Good enough with respect to what?" Even more important, ask her, "Good enough for whom?" Assure her that she is good enough for you. Tell her you are concerned about *her,* not about how much she weighs, what she eats, what she does, or how she looks.

2.  Help her become more independent. The bulimic needs to become more independent, that is, less dependent on pleasing others. You can be instrumental in this regard because you are probably one of the people she feels she must please.

Bulimic individuals are forever asking, "What should I do?" What many are really asking is, "What should I do in order to please you?" If possible, try not to answer this question. Rather, you might ask her what she wants to do. She is apt to respond by telling you what she *should* do, *must* do, or is *expected to* do. At that point, you can respond by saying, "No, I asked what you *wanted* to do." She is not used to focusing on what she wants, so she may not know. In this case, encourage her to try what she thinks she wants and reassure her that she is okay even if it does not work out well.

Noncontingent reinforcement can also be helpful in assisting the bulimic person to be less dependent on pleasing. By this, we mean showing your approval or acceptance without regard to what she might be doing. This can be done by letting her know you love, appreciate, and value her unconditionally. This does not mean, "I love (appreciate, value) you *because. . . ."* Rather, it simply means, "I love (appreciate, value) *you!"* These examples have been verbal. Obviously, nonverbal expressions (such as hugging, kissing, and touching) also work well either alone or with verbal expression.

Responding unconditionally is sometimes misinterpreted as, "You mean I have to accept everything she does no matter how much I disagree with it?" It is okay to dislike what she *does,* and it is okay to tell her this. But make a distinction for her between her and what she does. An example might be: "I love you but I very much dislike what you did."

Try to determine what role, if any, the individual's pleasing may play in her interactions with you. You may unknowingly be reinforcing or encouraging her dependent or pleasing behavior. For example, you may be responding positively to her athletic exploits when, in fact, she hates sports and is participating solely to please you. If you are able to discern that something like this is occurring, talk with her directly to clear up her misguided endeavor to please you. Let her know you are much more interested in how happy she is rather than in how well she performs.

Finally, because pleasing is so important, it might be helpful to talk with your bulimic friend or family member about pleasing you. Suggest to her that there is nothing wrong with pleasing people as long as it is not at her expense and that you like to be pleased as much as anyone. Most important, however, let her know that you will be most pleased when she is healthy and happy.

3.  Help her increase her tolerance for anxiety and frustration. Part of the bulimic's frustration and anxiety results from unrealistic expectations. She is apt to attribute some of these expectations to you. She is sometimes correct but sometimes wrong in her attributions. It would be helpful to her to know what your expectations really are. As you are recounting your expectations for her, attempt to discern how realistic they are in terms of what is expected during what period of time. Talk to her about modifications that will make expectations more realistic and how you might better provide the encouragement and support necessary to meet those expectations.

Part of the bulimic's difficulty in tolerating anxiety and frustration is that she is usually feeling a great deal of both. This is in part because she holds her feelings in. Encourage her to let these feelings out as she talks with you, thereby releasing some of her pent-up anxiety and frustration.

You may be able to change several things you are doing that frustrate the bulimic or make her anxious. Obviously, the best way to find out what these are is to ask. She is apt to be hesitant to tell you for fear of disapproval, so she will have to be urged and encouraged. Tell her you want to make changes that decrease her anxiety and frustration.

Finally, the bulimic may or may not tell you about the following sources of anxiety and frustration. The first is "pushing" food at her—this creates anxiety initially and eventually leads to frustration and anger. If she does not want to eat, do not push. Second, vigilantly watching her, trying to catch her bingeing or purging, makes her anxious. In fact, it may make her so anxious that it increases her bingeing and purging. Third, if you should accidently walk in on her bingeing or purging, it is recommended that you not try to stop her. Attempting to interrupt her is apt to create considerable frustration resulting in more bingeing and purging.

4. Deal with her compulsive behaviors. Compulsive behaviors are quite resistant to change, even for a therapist experienced in working with such behaviors. Other than encouraging the bulimic to do what she really wants rather than what she feels she should, there is not a great deal you can do to help with her compulsiveness, and for many reasons, it is probably better not to try. Compulsive behaviors are used to help the individual manage fear and anxiety. By attempting to alter these behaviors, you may succeed only in increasing her anxiety and frustration. It is probably better to simply be aware that the person is engaging in these behaviors. This lets you know that she is attempting to deal indirectly with something she is finding difficult. Once she has completed her compulsive ritual, you might inquire how she is feeling and if there is anything you can do to help.

5. Help her manage her irresponsibility. The bulimic should be held accountable for her irresponsibility. "Accountable," how-

ever, does not mean nagged, chastised, or punished. She typically nags, chastises, and punishes herself more than enough. Rather, it means confronting her or making her aware of her irresponsibility without being accusing or too critical. Accusations and criticism are apt to promote defensiveness, which interferes with good communication. Remember, she is not a bad person; in fact, some of her irresponsibility may indirectly result from trying to be too good. Your patience and understanding may be enhanced by recalling that some of her irresponsibility is due to fear and poor concentration.

If her irresponsible behavior appears to be a passive communication of anger, this behavior should be gently confronted. Ask her if she is angry. If she admits that she is, request that she be more direct and tell you what she is angry about.

Sometimes family and friends are *too* helpful with the bulimic's irresponsibility; that is, they take care of the problem for her. It is always advisable to be helpful through your support and encouragement—help her do what she needs to do but do not bail her out or do it for her. If you do it for her, she does not learn to be responsible but rather learns that you will rescue her.

6. How to handle her histrionic behavior. Usually, histrionic expressions are a result of not having one's feelings or behaviors attended to at less intense or extreme levels of expression. If you should notice what appears to be an exaggerated expression of emotion or behavior, suggest to her that she does not need to exaggerate or perform to get your attention. Rather, she should come to you and directly express how she is really feeling or request what she wants.

7. Help her make decisions. Much of what can be helpful here has already been discussed in previous sections; that is, encourage the bulimic to make her own decisions and to make them based on what she wants. Also, if she does not know what she wants or is afraid to decide, encourage her to experiment or take a risk. Reassure her that you will support her even if her decision does not turn out well.

8. Respond to her lying and stealing. Lying and stealing should be handled like other forms of irresponsible behavior. She

must be confronted and held accountable for her behavior. If she has taken food that does not belong to her, she should be expected to replace it within a twenty-four-hour time frame. If she takes money, she should replace it that day or work it off if she has no money.

9. Remember that personality traits are relatively enduring aspects of the individual and not easy to change. She may be able to modify her behavior some in ways that will be less self-defeating, but it is unrealistic to believe that she will be able to change long-standing characteristics of her personality without long-term treatment. This is an area upon which family and friends are *not* going to have very much impact or influence. However, overcoming bulimia does not necessarily require major changes in one's personality. A qualified specialist can provide some guidance in helping you handle irritating aspects of her personality as well as in helping you set realistic expectations for what might change and what probably will not.

A final note on changing long-standing personality styles involves the bulimic's belief that she cannot change. Often, she will become frustrated and tell herself that she cannot change, giving numerous explanations for why she is the way she is. On these occasions, it is important to remind her that these explanations only tell her why she is the way she is — they do not say she cannot change. Encourage her to think that she is not incapable of changing, but that she simply has not changed yet.

PART

III

# Understanding
# the Problem

Bulimia is a very complicated problem with three separate but interrelated parts. Understanding bulimia will be easier if you understand these three components: the behaviors involved (eating and purging); the thoughts or thinking patterns that are common among bulimics; and the emotions or feelings that bulimics are either avoiding or trying to deal with.

Each aspect of the problem affects, and is affected by, the others. More specifically, the way an individual thinks will affect how she behaves (eats) and how she feels. Likewise, how she eats will influence how she thinks about herself and how she feels. Finally, how she feels will affect how she eats and how she thinks.

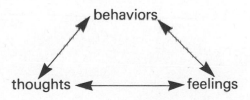

This cycle works against the individual when things are not going well. If she does not eat well, thinks negatively, or is feeling depressed, a negative cycle begins that strengthens itself each time the person goes through each step of the cycle. However, if an individual can change her thinking, then her eating and the way she feels will likely improve. Similarly, if she can change her eating, her thoughts and feelings are likely to be more positive also. Finally, if she is feeling better about herself, it is likely her thinking and eating behaviors will similarly be positive.

Treatment, therefore, focuses on bringing about changes in each of these critical aspects. While it is possible to see improvements when the treatment focus is solely on one aspect of the problem (since one aspect of the cycle serves to strengthen the others), we believe it is most effective to attend to all three aspects of the problem.

Chapters 5, 6, and 7 will elaborate on each of these three components. Understanding the complexity of what your daughter, spouse, or friend is experiencing will help you better understand bulimia. This understanding may also help *you* feel less frustrated and angry for what may have previously appeared to be only a sick or oppositional behavior.

At the end of each chapter you will find some specific suggestions for ways you might approach each aspect of bulimia — her bingeing and purging behaviors, her thoughts, and her emotions.

# 5

# Behaviors

## What Is Meant by the "Behavioral Part" of the Problem?

The behavioral part of the problem refers to all of the behaviors that contribute to and make up the problem of bulimia. These behaviors include binge-eating, vomiting, laxative abuse, diuretic (water pill) abuse, diet pill abuse, excessive exercise, and fasting. While the behaviors comprise only one-third of the problem (the thinking and emotional components will be discussed later), they are the easiest part of the problem to focus on because they are observable. Unfortunately, many bulimics and their families focus solely on the behaviors and, in so doing, miss the more significant issues of the eating disorder.

## Should We Talk to Her about Her Eating?

The only way to know whether or not to talk about eating is to ask her. Generally, the bulimic prefers not to talk about it. She may feel too embarrassed to talk with you about her eating. Additionally, she may spend her entire day thinking about, evaluating, and planning what she will eat, how and if she will purge, and how much she weighs. As a result, talking about eating often becomes boring, redundant, and irritating to her—it is a good way to turn her off. Carla is an excellent example. She became extremely angry and irritable if family members discussed her eating and purging with her. She interpreted their questions of concern as attempts to control her bingeing and purging.

Although Carla's response is typical of many bulimics, a few, like Michelle, prefer having family members ask about their eating. For Michelle, their asking meant that they cared and were concerned, and she very much needed and wanted their caring and concern.

Obviously, the range of the individual's response to your questions about eating is significantly large, as indicated by Carla and Michelle's responses. For this reason, it is important to ask her if she would find it helpful or problematic to talk about it. It is equally important to remember that even if she states that it is often helpful, there are apt to be times when she will nonetheless be upset by it. Thus, it is always imperative to approach the subject gently and with great sensitivity.

Even though you gently and sensitively ask her whether talking about her eating is acceptable, she may be noncommittal or simply reply, "I don't know." Remember from our discussion in chapter 4 that bulimics have difficulty making decisions for a variety of reasons. This may simply be another decision she cannot make. A general rule in this instance is not to talk with her about it unless she brings it up. By adopting this rule, you reduce the risk of upsetting an individual who is probably already feeling bad.

A final note on talking about the bulimic's eating concerns whether or not it is helpful to talk with her about it even if she wants to. She already places too much importance on her eating and weight. If we talk with her about it too frequently, too long, or too seriously, we are apt to help her believe that her eating and weight are as important as she mistakenly believes they are. It is probably best to deal with her eating and weight concerns in as expeditious a manner as sensitive communication will allow. Then redirect the conversation to more salient areas of her life, such as health, happiness, family, relationships, job, or school. More specifically, talk with her about *her*—who she is, how she feels, and what is important to her. These are more normal areas to talk about than eating, weight, and food. As such, they assist in feeling more normal. Finally, regardless of what you talk with her about, it is important that you talk *with* her rather than *at* her. "Talking at" implies lecturing, whereas "talking with" implies a more normal give-and-take communication.

## How Should We Handle Eating at Home?

Allow the bulimic as much control as is feasible with regard to food shopping, meal planning, and meal preparation. This is not to say that she should make all the decisions in these areas. However, she needs to be involved in them.

Try not to watch her eat. It is hard not to watch the eating of someone you care about who has an eating disorder, but watching will only put pressure on her. Actually, most people report feeling uncomfortable when others watch them eat. The bulimic individual is already anxious and uncomfortable with eating; making her more so is the last thing we want to do. And most important, do *not* follow her to the bathroom after she eats—do not try to catch her vomiting. That kind of vigilance only brings about anger, resentment, and mistrust. You cannot stop her from bingeing and purging once she has decided to do it, and attempting to prevent her will only lead to more bingeing and purging.

## What Is a Binge Food?

A binge food varies with the individual. The concept of a binge food can probably best be understood after a brief discussion of what constitutes a binge. Like the term "binge food," the term "binge" is also variable. For one person, a binge might be ingesting a large volume of food, such as 5000 calories. For another, it is simply eating food that the person feels she should not eat. For another, it is eating calories that put her over her allotted level as dictated by her diet. Perhaps the most interesting definition of a binge came from a thirty-four-year-old mother who defined a binge as "any eating that was followed by vomiting."

A *binge food* is typically a food that either constitutes a binge when eaten or triggers a binge-eating episode. Most people assume a binge food is a sweet food, and often this is the case. However, any food — even salad — can be a binge food or trigger a binge. Interestingly, many of our patients have either binged or begun a binge by eating cereal, a food often believed to be healthy and safe. *Safe foods* are typically foods that are either low in calories or are not believed to be a trigger for binge-eating.

## Should We Not Keep Binge Foods in the House?

This should be a family decision. Keeping binge foods out of the house will not prevent bingeing — it may simply make it more difficult or less convenient. If the bulimic requests this and other family members are not strongly opposed, then the decision not to have binge foods in the house is fine; but it should be made for a short time only because other family members may feel deprived, thus creating resentment. Eating-disordered families usually have enough negative feelings to deal with without adding more. These foods are a part of the real world, and the bulimic individual must at some point deal with them. In actuality, it is not really the foods that she is afraid of. Rather, it is her fear that she cannot eat them or perhaps even be around them without going out of control and eating too much.

Marsha at age seventeen was living at home with her parents and two younger siblings. The family regularly bought cookies for everyone to eat. Unfortunately, Marsha found these cookies to be an almost irresistible binge food. At one family session, we discussed the problem. Other family members wanted to be able to have cookies in the house. A compromise was reached in that the family agreed to purchase Marsha's least favorite cookies.

## What Should We Do about Large Amounts of Food "Disappearing"?

The individual must be held accountable. She needs to be confronted, but accountability and confrontation should not be critical or harsh. Punishment is not only unhelpful, it could be harmful. She knows she has acted inappropriately and feels bad. She also has probably already chastised and punished herself. Let her know, however, that it is her responsibility to replace the food she has binged on in a reasonable period of time. If she does not have the money necessary to replace the food, she must make arrangements to obtain it. Do not take responsibility for her by replacing the food or giving her the money necessary for replacement. It is always important in dealing with the bulimic to be as sensitive and understanding as possible. However, we recommend that she not be "let off the hook" unless very special extenuating circumstances warrant it.

## Can We Structure Mealtimes in a Way that Would Be Helpful?

Providing a relaxing environment for mealtimes can be helpful. In some families, mealtime may be the only time each day that the family is together. It can either be a relaxing and enjoyable time or a stressful one. Some of our patients report dinner as a time in which they are asked about any problems that have occurred during the day. The bulimic already feels uncomfortable with eating. The discussion of problems related to the family or the eating-disordered individual may add to her discomfort. We want to make eating as easy, comfortable, and enjoyable for her as possible. If she feels relaxed, she is apt to feel more in control psychologically and have an easier time eating normally. Consequently, problems that need to be addressed are probably best handled away from the dining table.

A general rule in assisting the bulimic individual with her eating is to try to arrange eating in such a manner that it in no way resembles bingeing. We have talked about making eating more relaxed (bingeing is typically stressed and fast). Another suggestion might include eating only well-prepared, nutritious food in an appropriate eating place, while sitting at a table with eating utensils. This eating arrangement contrasts favorably with bingeing, which often involves quickly eating prepackaged foods while standing or driving. It can also be helpful to the bulimic individual to eat without other activities going on, such as watching TV or reading.

Unfortunately, some of our patients report there are no mealtimes in their families. Eating may be a haphazard time when each person simply grabs what is available, or the family may eat out most of the time. The bulimic individual needs a structure to help her feel more in control. Cheryl came from a broken family and was not always in the same home at mealtime; even when she was, her relatives seldom cooked—cooked meals at home simply were not a part of her life. Consequently, it was difficult for her to practice appropriate eating behaviors or to plan meals at home.

## Do Meals Have to Occur at Specific Times Each Day?

A flexible schedule is helpful. The key words here are "schedule" and "flexible." A schedule can be helpful because it provides a structure that tells the person it is time to eat. A bulimic individual has lost a real sense of hunger. Many bulimics do not know when they are hungry or believe they are hungry all the time. Consequently, it is difficult for a bulimic person to eat only when she is hungry. A schedule allows the body to normalize; that is, through repeated practice of eating breakfast, lunch, and dinner, the body will at some point begin to send hunger signals to the individual that she is better able to trust. A schedule also gives the person some idea as to where the desire to eat is coming from. If it has only been an hour since she last ate (providing she ate enough), she can probably assume her desire to eat is not a hunger signal. If it has been six hours since she last ate, she can probably be more certain she is hungry.

A schedule is important, but flexibility within that schedule is equally important. Rigidity in the schedule will only increase tension and perhaps make the bulimic individual more compulsive. Again, we want to make eating easier and more pleasant. In planning meals, ask her when she would like to eat or what would be convenient for her, as long as it does not inconvenience other family members. Also, while it might be nice for everyone to eat together, it is not necessary for all family members to always eat together at the same time every day.

Finally, the flexible schedule needs to take the length of time between meals into consideration. Much of the binge-eating the bulimic does comes as a result of not eating. Current research in the area of eating disorders indicates that restrictive dieting leads to bingeing. That is, when we are overly hungry, we are much more likely to binge. Consequently, the effectiveness of a flexible eating schedule can be enhanced by ensuring that the individual will not go for long periods without eating.

## Why Does She Binge If She Wants to be Thin?

The individual usually binges due to psychological factors, physiological factors, or a combination of both. Psychologically, she may eat or overeat because she has been depriving herself of foods that she really wants to eat but will not allow herself to eat. Through a "reactance" process, she comes to want to eat the forbidden foods even more, often to the point of bingeing. We can all agree that when something is taken away or is unattainable, we tend to want and need it more. For example, if for some reason the water in your home were turned off, you would be apt to get thirsty, and water would likely become much more important to you. Similarly, foods we cannot have become very important — so important that we begin to think about them more, sometimes to the point of obsessing about them. These obsessions often lead to the eating of the forbidden foods.

Also, from a psychological point of view, bingeing is the bulimic's way of dealing with unpleasant emotions. As we have mentioned previously, the bulimic usually does not feel free to express her feelings. Holding onto her feelings, however, leads her to feel tense, anxious, and frustrated. Bingeing and purging are probably helpful in two ways. First, these behaviors provide a distraction from her uncomfortable feelings. Second, bingeing and purging allow her to release some of the tension that has built up from holding back her feelings. The bulimic experiences a sense of relief as this tension is released. She may also feel calmer and more in control, at least temporarily.

From a physiological point of view, dieting or food deprivation at some point creates biological pressure toward binge-eating. Recent research indicates that dieting leads to binge-eating. When the individual diets, especially when dieting is stringent, there is a biological need to eat. The body interprets strict dieting as starvation and counters this by signaling hunger and a need to eat. Additionally, most bulimics are restrained eaters. A *restrained eater* is an individual who actively diets and finds it difficult to give up enough control to eat. When she does, she is apt to give up *all* control and overeat. Suffice it to say that intense hunger leads the person to give up enough control to begin eating; restraint is then given up totally and bingeing occurs. Obviously, the combination of psychological and biological pressure on the bulimic individual who is forever dieting makes binge-eating highly probable if not inevitable.

One final point concerns the enjoyment derived from bingeing. Many bulimics think that they will enjoy the binge, but afterwards find it void of enjoyment. For those who do find enjoyment, it can probably be attributed to one of two factors. First, some report they actually enjoy the taste of the food. These are typically individuals who radically restrict their food intake, sometimes to the point that their bingeing is their only eating. They also tend to overrestrict other aspects of their lives, leaving little other than bingeing. Shelly, a patient in treatment at the time of this writing, is an excellent example. She is resisting making changes with her eating because she does not want to give up bingeing, which she reports enjoying very much. However, she eats very little other than bingeing. What she does eat tends to be quite bland (i.e., raw vegetables, popcorn, etc.). She also does virtually nothing other than bingeing, with working at a boring job the only exception. Her bingeing probably is the most enjoyable part of her life. And it is unrealistic to believe she will give it up as long as this is the case.

The second factor that affects the enjoyment associated with bingeing involves control, or more specifically, the release of tension. In order to binge, the bulimic must give up her tight restraint over her feelings and her eating. This release of restraint provides a tension release that is perceived as pleasurable. Some bulimics mistakenly attribute this pleasure to the bingeing rather than to the tension release. Obviously, the sense of relief or pleasure she believes has come as a result of bingeing and purging only helps maintain bulimia.

## Should We Comment on Weight Gain?

Typically, the answer is "no." The individual must stop dieting in order to get over her problem. Comments about weight imply that dieting and weight are the significant concerns, when in fact health and healthy eating are the goals. Nonetheless, the bulimic individual will probably be concerned about her weight and will most likely notice any weight gain without it being called to her attention. It is certainly alright to talk about weight with her if she brings up the topic. You might help her understand that some weight gain may occur as she is attempting to eat more normally. Very often some if not all of this weight is due to rebound water retention, which will dissipate over time. It may also take her metabolism time to adjust to eating normally. However, encourage her to stay with her new eating plan, and try to be patient. Reassure her that it is her health and happiness and not her weight that are of primary importance.

## Why is Weighing Such a Sensitive Issue?

It is true that most bulimic individuals are extremely sensitive about their weight, and many emotions such as fear and anxiety become associated with weighing. As a result, the bulimic assumes that her fear and anxiety are due to her weight and eating when in fact they are due to more significant issues in her life. Some bulimics respond to this fear and anxiety by staying away from scales and simply refusing to ever weigh themselves. Others have the opposite response and weigh themselves many times a day. Some patients have told us that they travel with their scale and wouldn't go anywhere without it. This all-or-nothing response is typical of the bulimic. Obviously, neither extreme is helpful; in fact, both are unhelpful.

Actually, weighing (or not weighing) becomes very important because it is often used to help manage unpleasant or uncomfortable emotions. Consequently, when the nonweighing bulimic is asked to weigh or the frequent-weighing bulimic is prevented from weighing, these unpleasant, uncomfortable emotions increase.

In that weighing is such a sensitive and complex issue for most bulimics, its modification is probably best left to a therapist in most cases. If in the unlikely event your bulimic friend or family member seeks your assistance with her weighing, there are some general guidelines you might follow. For the bulimic who is afraid to weigh (and in all likelihood is not weighing at all), try to encourage and support her enough that she will begin weighing once per week. Reassure her that whatever the scales say, you will help her deal with it, and more important, that you care about *her*—not what she weighs. Indicate to her that she is not weighing to see how much she weighs because her absolute weight is not particularly important. Rather, suggest to her that by weighing she can know if her weight is going up, going down, or staying the same and that not knowing at all is worse than knowing the worst: that she has gained weight. When she is not weighing, she usually assumes that she is either gaining or is too fat. At least by weighing, she will know what is happening and can do what is necessary as a result. Additionally, weighing obviously has great significance for her. Ask her what it means to her; talking about its meaning may allow her to let go of some of the emotion tied up with it. Initially, she may get on the scales and not want to know how much she weighs. This is okay for a while, but it means you will need to weigh her. Eventually, however, she will need to be able to weigh herself if for no other reason than to get over another irrational fear.

Additionally, because of the nonweighing bulimic's fear of weighing, it is important that she weigh in such a fashion that variations in weight due to nonnutritional factors are kept at a minimum. By this we mean she should weigh on the same scale at approximately the same time of day every week to avoid emotion that might be evoked as a result of misunderstanding normal daily fluctuations in weight.

As difficult as it is to change the nonweighing bulimic's behavior, it is perhaps even more difficult to alter the weighing behavior of the individual who is weighing too frequently; this person is actually afraid *not* to weigh. Consequently, great care and sensitivity must be used in assisting her to decrease her weighing behaviors. Try to remember that she believes the likelihood of becoming fat is less if she weighs frequently; it is almost as if she believes the fat will creep or jump on her body without her vigilantly monitoring it. To minimize her discomfort, encourage her to slowly decrease the number of weighings. For example, if she is weighing six times a day, suggest that she try weighing only five times a day for a few days. If successful, then she can try decreasing it to four times a day for a few days, and so on.

Remember that weighing for this individual is being used to manage fear and anxiety. That is, she feels less fear and anxiety when she weighs frequently because she is able to reassure herself that she has not gained weight. Consequently, when she decreases her weighing, she is apt to feel these emotions more intensely. Try to support her at these times. Help her understand that she was already feeling anxious and afraid and that weighing was simply distracting her from these feelings. Encourage her to talk with you about these feelings or to express them through writing when you are not available.

As we mentioned earlier, weighing is a very sensitive issue for the bulimic. Unless she asks for your assistance, weighing is best left to a therapist. Even if she asks, however, do not push weighing or not weighing. If she resists your efforts or becomes upset, gently back off.

## Why Does She Purge?

Purging can serve many purposes. First, purging is a way the bulimic individual attempts to undo her eating. Because she does not want to gain weight from her bingeing, she tries to remove the weight-gain potential from food by inducing vomiting, abusing laxatives, abusing diuretics, or through any combination of these purgation methods. Purging also allows for an emotional release. As the tension associated with holding back emotion increases, the need to release this tension also increases. The release of pent-up emotion, as well as the relief of emptying an over-stuffed stomach, greatly reinforce purging behaviors. Many bulimics believe that their bingeing and purging are signs that they are out of control. However, purging actually signals the end of a difficult, stressful process that allows the individual to once again feel in control, if only for a short period. The sense of being in control can also reinforce purging.

Purging is actually more destructive than bingeing. Physiologically, it will dehydrate the body and can create an electrolyte imbalance. Psychologically, it reinforces the bingeing. When the individual feels she has undone the bingeing, she actually increases the likelihood that she will binge again. She has, in essence, made it "okay" because she believes she will not gain weight now that she has taken care of the food. Many bulimics actually tell themselves it is okay to binge because they can always throw it up.

Although most of our discussion of purging has focused on vomiting as well as laxative and diuretic abuse, fasting and excessive exercise may also play a purgative role for the bulimic. These behaviors differ in that they can be used before as well as after bingeing; that is, she may legitimize a binge through fasting or exercise. More specifically, if the person knows she is going out to eat or will be in a situation where she will be expected to eat, she may fast all day, exercise excessively, or abuse laxatives or diuretics to make the eating okay. Purging before eating is used to make eating acceptable, while purging afterward is used to undo the eating. In either case, purging is used to nullify the potential weight gain resulting from eating.

Ellen, a college sophomore, provides an excellent example of an individual who purged before eating. Obviously, purging at many social functions would not be possible without the threat of detection. Whenever Ellen had a date or social plans that included eating but precluded purging after eating, she would purge beforehand by fasting all day and exercising excessively. Only then did she feel she was safe in eating—that is, did not have to fear weight gain.

## What Should Be Done about Messy Bathrooms?

Our recommendation here is much the same as for eating large volumes of food—accountability and responsibility. If her vomiting is responsible for the mess, it is her responsibility to clean it up. Again, sensitivity is needed in holding the individual responsible. In fact, more sensitivity and understanding may be necessary. As embarrassed as she may be over being confronted with bingeing, she may feel humiliated regarding her vomiting. It is important that she not feel she is being punished for vomiting. Rather, she needs to know she is simply being asked to be responsible by cleaning up after herself.

## Why Would She Use Laxatives or Diuretics to Control Her Weight?

Laxatives and diuretics help the bulimic individual believe she is losing weight. Actually, both simply remove water from the body. Although the use of laxatives and diuretics promotes temporary water weight loss, this practice also sets up and maintains a cycle of water loss followed by rebound water retention. This rebound water retention, a process in which the body actually overfills and creates bloating, is probably the single most frequent complaint of the bulimic. This bloating is so uncomfortable that the bulimic will again resort to laxatives, diuretics, or vomiting in a futile effort to lose the water to feel thinner. Of course, the body then rebounds with water retention and the process begins again.

Although the bulimic complains of bloating, the primary difficulties associated with laxative and diuretic abuse, as well as vomiting, are potentially much more serious. The rapid removal of water from the body often creates an electrolyte imbalance. Electrolytes—potassium, sodium, and chloride ions—are necessary for proper functioning of the body's major systems. Long-term abuse of laxatives or diuretics can lead to significant heart, kidney, and liver dysfunction and in extreme cases even to death (see chapter 1).

Extensive laxative abuse can also lead to a "lazy" digestive tract that may refuse to function without laxatives, thereby setting up a cycle of laxative abuse followed by constipation followed again by laxative abuse. The bulimic individual also tends to develop a tolerance to laxatives and may need to increase her dosage in order to derive the desired effect. While two or four laxatives may work initially, many bulimics increase their dose when the previous amount stops working for them. One patient of ours who had abused laxatives for years came to us after taking fifty to sixty laxatives at a time. Obviously, medicine of any type can be dangerous when taken in large quantities; laxatives are no exception.

## Is It Wrong for Her to Want to Lose Weight?

It is not wrong to want to lose weight if there is a real need to lose. The desire to lose weight in the absence of a real need, however, suggests that the individual, at best, feels tremendous sociocultural pressures to be thin or, at worst, may have an emotional problem. Additionally, the intensity of the desire is important. Obviously, the individual who simply wants to reduce the amount of fatty foods she is eating is different from the individual who very compulsively measures every morsel of food she ingests. Usually, greater intensity, time, and worry involved with the desire suggest an emotional problem.

Many bulimic individuals do not need to lose weight; that is, they are not really overweight. The desire to lose weight can be used by the bulimic individual to distract herself from her emotions and the significant issues in her life. If the individual is overweight, direct attempts at weight loss should be postponed until she is over her bulimia. It is highly improbable that she can lose weight safely and effectively while she is bulimic. More importantly, it is unlikely if not impossible for her to get over her bulimia as long as she is dieting. Interestingly, many bulimics lose weight as a by-product of getting well. Often bingeing and purging are responsible for weight gain. As a result, the bulimic person frequently loses weight (especially if she is overweight) when she controls her bingeing and purging.

Weight loss is not only wrong when unnecessary but may even

be dangerous. Unfortunately, weight loss can be dangerous for many when it includes a loss of vital proteins. The importance of protein involves both the issues of dieting and the result of dieting. Many people who diet do not get enough protein—they often avoid foods that are protein-dense because of the calories they contain. Not getting enough protein is bad enough when calorie levels are normal; it is worse when intake levels are reduced below those necessary for energy balance (balance between calories ingested and calories burned). Typically, when people diet, carbohydrate and fat intake is reduced. Thus, the energy provided by carbohydrates and fats is reduced; this reduction in energy forces proteins into more of an energy-related function, leaving other necessary bodily processes without the amino acids they need to function. One of these processes involves the maintenance of lean tissue, and we never want to lose lean tissue. Both the loss of protein and its inadequate ingestion during dieting result in lean tissue loss. Protein also plays vital roles in water regulation, menstrual functioning, metabolism, fighting infection, digestion, and, of course, building muscle and other body tissue.

In concluding this section, we would like to clarify some of our issues regarding dieting. When we use the term "dieting," we are referring to a process that centers primarily on strict calorie restriction. We do not favor dieting for most nonbulimic people because it is not usually an effective way to lose weight and maintain weight loss, not to mention that some diets may be harmful to some people. We are even more opposed to dieting for the majority of the bulimics we work with. The bulimia began with dieting in most cases, and dieting makes recovery impossible. Dieting after treatment would also be a mistake in the majority of cases. In fact, if the individual still has a strong wish to lose weight after treatment, she has probably not really gotten over her eating problem.

## What Can We Do to Help?

1. Focus less on her behaviors (eating, bingeing, vomiting, laxative or diuretic use, exercise, etc.) and more on how she feels.

Too much emphasis on behaviors can reinforce the bulimic's use of behaviors as distractions from her emotional state. That is, eating or weight-related behaviors or symptoms will distract her from her feelings. Focusing on those behaviors allows her to avoid dealing with the crux of the problem — the feelings that generate these protective distractions. But do not mistake our admonitions regarding talking about food as a recommendation not to talk; nothing could be further from the truth. First, talk *with* her and, second, talk with her about whatever is on *her* mind. Of course, it is always recommended to talk with her about what is really important in her life, such as her health, happiness, school, job, and relationships.

2.  Do *not* follow her to the bathroom or try to catch her in the act when she is purging. If she tells you she has binged or purged, try not to panic. Of course, you are concerned, and it is this concern that you want to convey. Try not to be judgmental. She knows she has done something she should not have and she feels bad about it; she is already judging herself. Judging is not what she needs — what she needs is understanding. Talk with her about how she is feeling. For example, she may feel afraid or depressed. Ask her how you can help and then try to do what she suggests. An example might be, "You seem depressed (anxious, afraid, upset, etc.); is there anything I can do to help?"

3.  Make mealtimes sociable and enjoyable. It is a time for family and friends to get together. It is not a time to focus on mistakes made that day or to question someone about her eating or lack thereof. Try to use this time to relax and enjoy being together. Most serious matters that require discussion can wait until after mealtime. The relaxation and enjoyment of eating together can be enhanced by making sure mealtimes are set aside for the family and enough time is made available so it is not a rushed experience. Finally, although many of our patients report eating as a difficult or stressful experience, they also tell us that eating with others can be helpful; having others with them when they eat can help them feel more in control, especially when they feel no demands from others regarding their eating. Eating with others is also helpful

in that it is more normal, while eating alone is more reminiscent of bingeing.

4. Encourage the bulimic individual to help in the meal planning and preparation. Knowing what is in the food and how it is prepared will allow her to feel more in control. If she can have some control over her own meals, she may not need to fear mealtime.

5. If your bulimic friend or family member trusts you enough to ask for your assistance when she is feeling as though she needs or wants to binge and purge, then there are ways you might be helpful. Most important, you can simply talk with her. Try to support her; ask her how she is feeling; let her talk; but try to help her stay focused on her feelings. An additional helpful strategy might include suggesting alternative behaviors or activities to bingeing and purging. Good alternatives would include almost any behavior that would be healthy, enjoyable, or relaxing for her. Assist her in compiling a list of such alternatives that she can consult when anticipating a binge and purge episode.

6. Know your limitations and responsibilities. Bulimia is a very emotionally charged disorder, both for the individual and for those who are significant in her life. It is a disorder that makes others feel they should do something; the anxiety, fear, and sometimes anger on the part of those concerned about the bulimic individual often push them to act or to at least feel that they should act. But you cannot stop her from bingeing and purging, nor are you responsible for her bingeing and purging. She may have feelings about you that help her be bulimic, but *she* is responsible for them and *she* is responsible for her bingeing and purging. Your responsibility is to listen and try to understand her in an effort to be helpful to her. She must stop her bingeing and purging, but you may be able to help her stop through your support, encouragement, and concern. However, even with proper assistance from those who care about her, the individual will still have a difficult time giving up her disorder. Bulimia is a very difficult problem to get over; the bulimic must be ready to give it up and be willing to work hard and take the necessary risks in treat-

ment in order to get well. Suffice it to say, it is not your fault if she does not get well.

7.  Try to avoid a power struggle over food. Power struggles are apt to occur with a disorder like bulimia. The bulimic may use her bingeing and purging as a way to feel more in control or to challenge other power bases such as friends or family. Try to resist her need to challenge. If you respond by joining her in a struggle for power, her problem is apt to worsen. A patient of ours provides an illustrative example. Cathy was a high school student who lived with her grandmother. When her grandmother was aware of Cathy bingeing and purging, she would deny her access to food in the house, saying that she would not be allowed to eat because she was just going to throw up the food anyway. Obviously, this placed Cathy in a precarious bind; it helped her want to binge just to get back at her grandmother. It also made it harder for her to eat and easier for her not to eat — neither of which were helpful to her. Even if she ate with no intention to binge, she still ran the risk of evoking her grandmother's wrath.

    If you are angry with a bulimic friend or relative, be direct and talk with her about your anger. Try to avoid using food or her eating as a way to be angry with her; this simply places more importance in an area that the bulimic has already made too important. It must be remembered that it is easy for her to mistake your anger or concern as control, and control is the primary issue for her. Let her know that you are not interested in controlling her but in helping her feel more in control.

# 6

# Thoughts

## What Role Does Thinking Play in Bulimia?

Thinking is sometimes referred to as the "cognitive" part of the problem. The behaviors (eating and purging) and the emotions comprise the remaining parts of the bulimia equation. But these three components do not operate in isolation; rather, they greatly affect each other. That is, the way one thinks has a great deal to do with how one feels and what one does.

Thinking is actually self-talk. Probably everyone knows at least one positive thinker and at least one negative thinker. In most instances, these two individuals will respond in very different ways to the same situations. This is based, in part, on the self-statements they make. Therefore, the negative thinker who tells herself that she will fail is likely to have lower self-esteem and be less willing to make an effort to do what she wants or needs than the positive thinker. The bulimic engages in this type of negative thinking, which helps maintain the problem.

## What Types of Thoughts or Self-Statements Do Bulimics Have?

Bulimics often engage in both irrational thinking and in rationalizations. Irrational thoughts are inaccuracies in thinking. These illogical thoughts, or distortions, cause us to believe things about ourselves and what we do that are not based in reality. These distortions also serve to maintain both bulimia and depression by helping the person exaggerate the likelihood and intensity of negative outcomes as well as by reinforcing a negative self-image and self-esteem. Due to low self-esteem, the bulimic tells herself that she cannot achieve anything. As a result, she decides not to try. Because she does not try, she cannot accomplish anything. Because she does not accomplish anything, she feels like a failure, and the cycle begins again.

When irrational thoughts are taken one step further to justify actions, the individual is engaging in rationalization. Rationalization (not to be confused with rational thinking) is a cognitive process whereby the individual makes a thought or behavior appear reasonable, rational, or logical when in actuality it is not. It justifies or legitimizes an irrational act or idea. Bulimics may use rationalization to justify binge-eating or to justify not eating.

**What are examples of irrational thoughts?**  The following examples are an adaptation from a book by David Burns called *Feeling Good.*

**All-or-nothing thinking.** This is one of the bulimic's most common thinking errors. It occurs when an individual sees things in concrete, absolute, black-and-white categories. When the bulimic does not eat perfectly, she sees herself as a total failure. Jan is a typical example. To her, a person is either thin or fat. Because she does not view herself as being thin, she must be fat. In order for Jan to get well, she must be able to find some moderation in her thinking and conceptualizations.

**Overgeneralization.** This occurs when an individual uses one mistake to predict that she will never change. The bulimic may use one binge episode to predict that she will never be able to eat normally. Melissa provides an illustrative example. Despite the fact that she had eaten normally on many if not most occasions, one binge and purge episode would lead her to believe that she may as well give up on getting well; at these times, she told herself that she would never be a normal eater. In fact, she will not become a normal eater unless she can be aware of, and rebut, her overgeneralizations regarding her eating.

**Disqualifying the positive.** In this case an individual rejects positive experiences or things done well by telling herself that they "don't count." The bulimic, for example, "doesn't count" any of her positive eating experiences. Six weeks into treatment, Diane, a thirty-year-old mother of two, negatively expressed that she was a failure with her treatment and that she could not get well. When encouraged to actually count her positive versus negative eating experiences since beginning treatment, Diane became aware that sixty of sixty-two eating experiences had been positive. However, she had chosen through her distorted thinking to focus on the two negative ones rather than on the sixty positive ones. Making her aware of this distortion was only the first step in changing her maladaptive thinking; she then had to be taught how to respond to herself in a way that was more helpful and accurate.

**Jumping to conclusions.** This occurs when one quickly interprets an experience negatively even when there are no facts to support that evaluation or assumption. The bulimic may convince herself that she will not be able to eat appropriately when in fact she has done so many times. One patient told us that she felt she had to skip parties because she might binge-eat while there. This fear was based on an experience in which she probably had too much to eat and assumed that everyone had noticed. Interestingly, this person would not allow herself to go to parties but would later become angry and depressed and would binge-eat at home. Unfortunately, she would then tell herself that she was right not to have gone because she would have binged.

**Magnification and minimization.** This involves exaggerating one's own mistakes (with eating, for example) while minimizing the mistakes and failures of others. It is okay for others to be overweight, but for the bulimic it is viewed as catastrophic. This was evidenced in one group by a patient named Julie, who could be positive and supportive of other therapy group members when they made mistakes with their eating, but who would greatly exaggerate her own eating mistakes.

**Emotional reasoning.** This occurs when an individual believes that her negative feeling accurately reflects how things really are. The bulimic may *feel* awful and, therefore, assumes she must *be* awful. Or she may feel fat and thereby assume she *is* fat. The following example comes from a college student named Susan. Susan was not fat; in fact, she was slightly underweight. However, when she felt depressed, she felt "heavy," which translated to "fat" for her. So rather than saying she felt depressed, she would state to herself and to others that she felt fat. Because she felt fat, she assumed she was fat when in fact she was depressed.

**Should statements.** The individual uses "shoulds" in an attempt to motivate herself. For example, she might tell herself, "I *should* always be in control of my eating." In actuality, this process results in her feeling guilty or frustrated. "Shoulds" almost always imply pressure. The bulimic may pressure herself by telling herself that she should be able to eat better. Many patients talk to us about their beliefs that they should be perfect eaters as well as perfect in all other ways.

Imagine spending most of your day thinking in the ways just described above. Further imagine that you are an individual with low self-esteem. Repeatedly telling yourself that you are "fat," "no good," "bad," "hopeless," "a failure," and so forth can only lead to depression and further low self-esteem. These thoughts and feelings lead the bulimic to use food to alleviate, if only temporarily, her discomfort.

## What Are Some Typical Rationalizations Bulimics Use?

### "IF I START EATING, I WON'T BE ABLE TO STOP."

While the bulimic individual agrees with this statement, it is obviously false in that no one continuously eats. What she is really saying is that she is afraid she will not stop eating as soon as she thinks she should. But that is not what she tells herself. Rather, she tells herself that she will not be able to stop. And she tells herself this often enough so that she believes it. But she does not eat when she is sleeping or when she is taking a shower, for example. She does not eat during our therapy sessions. Despite the evidence that she can control her eating, she uses this statement as a way to try to convince herself not to eat. In essence, she attempts to scare herself away from food. Unfortunately, staying away from food or skipping meals only increases the chances that she will binge later. She actually creates the situation she fears. Also, each time she binges, she further convinces herself that she cannot control her eating.

### "If I Don't Get Rid of What I Eat, I'll Get Fat."

The bulimic believes that any food that stays in her body will turn to fat. What she tells herself is that she cannot eat normally without getting fat. There are numerous inaccuracies in this statement. First, she believes she cannot eat without gaining weight. She associates eating with gaining weight. Obviously, not all eating leads to weight gain. She also believes that any weight she gains must be fat, which also is not accurate. Some weight can be fat but other weight may be lean muscle mass or fluid. She is also making a statement regarding eating normally. First of all, many bulimics do not know what normal eating is. And second, many bulimics have eaten abnormally for so long that an adequate test of normal eating has not been tried in recent months or years.

Actually, when bulimics begin to eat three meals a day and learn to control their bingeing and purging, many lose small amounts of weight, especially if they are overweight. This occurs for several reasons. First, food that is ingested is not totally regurgitated; that is, some of the food remains in the stomach. Often this is high calorie food. Second, vomiting dehydrates the body. The body then overfills through a process referred to as rebound water retention, which adds water weight. Finally, the unusual eating of the bulimic alters her metabolism, making weight gain easier. Normal eating removes water retention, normalizes her metabolism, and resets the satiety signal (lets her know when she is full)—all of which may promote weight loss.

### "I'm Too Fat—I'm Disgusting."

While this is a dominant thought, it goes much further than that. It goes something like this: "I am too fat, therefore no one will love me, therefore I will be alone and unhappy." The real fallacy

for many bulimics is that they are not fat, that is, noticeably overweight. In fact, many are slightly underweight. The bulimic is
obviously an unhappy individual. An extension of the fat fallacy
is that she assumes that she would be happier if she could just be
thinner. Bulimics assume that their unhappiness is due to the fact
that they are fat. Of course, this kind of thinking is really a distraction that keeps them from discovering the real sources of
their unhappiness. You may be wondering why the bulimic would
focus on her weight rather than other aspects of her life if she is
unhappy. The answer to this question probably lies in the emphasis placed on thinness in our society. We receive constant
messages from the print and visual media that we must be thin in
order to be happy, accepted, and loved. So if the young woman
is unhappy, she can attribute it to her weight; that is, "I would be
so much happier if I could just lose that last ten pounds." The real
danger here is that even if she can lose the weight she will still not
be happy. And she will assume that she is still fat and needs to
lose more.

## "I've Already Eaten This Much — I May as Well Eat the Whole Thing."

This rationalization is the one that is probably used more often
by more bulimics than any other. It is also the one that makes the
least sense to the family member or friend who is attempting to
understand and help the bulimic. Let's break down this rationalization and see if we can make it more understandable. First, the
initial part of the rationalization ("I've already eaten this much")
is true; that is, she has already eaten this much. The truth in the
first part then helps the bulimic believe the second part without
really thinking about it — at least without thinking about it *rationally*. The second part of the rationalization ("I may as well eat the
whole thing") is not rational; that is, it does not *logically* follow. To
people trying to understand the bulimic, it makes little sense to
eat more after determining that too much has already been eaten.
We must remember, however, that the bulimic is not working
from a rational, logical position that makes sense. She is being
driven by emotion. What she thinks makes sense to her.

As discussed earlier, the bulimic individual thinks in an all-
or-nothing fashion. Once she believes she has eaten too much, it

is as if she has flipped a switch. The control that was "on" is now "off." She gives up any remaining eating control, reasoning that her eating is no longer perfect so it may as well be as bad as it can be. This "reasoning" allows her to eat all she wants, but it is also related to purging. Obviously, the more she eats, the more she will need to purge in order to remove stomach discomfort and threat of weight gain. Additionally, purging is reportedly easier when the stomach is full. Consequently, this type of thinking increases the legitimacy and likelihood of bingeing *and* purging.

### "I'VE HAD A BAD DAY; I DESERVE TO EAT WHATEVER I WANT."

This rationalization is somewhat different than the previous ones in that both parts of this statement are true. The life of the bulimic is quite difficult, and she almost always deprives herself of what she needs and wants. It is the two parts taken together that constitutes the irrationality. Even though McDonald's tells us, "You deserve a break today," it does not logically follow that over-eating is a reasonable way to deal with having a bad day. As we have discussed previously, however, the bulimic individual is not being rational or logical; she is attempting to deal with her uncomfortable emotions in the best way she knows how; unfortunately, the best way she has learned to that point is bingeing and purging.

The notion of "deserving" represents a problem for the bulimic. Many bulimics often believe that they do not deserve to eat. Obviously, eating is not a behavior that is deserved in the sense that it is earned, but many bulimics think differently. They often think that they deserve to eat only when their eating has been good, or after exercise, or following periods of dieting or fasting. This sense of deserving can be taken a step further. The individual may be so down on herself that she does not believe she deserves to eat because she is such a bad person; in essence, it is punishment through deprivation. This idea was carried to such an extreme by one of our patients that she denied herself water in addition to food.

How does the bulimic associate feeling bad and deserving to eat what she wants? It is always difficult to discern where beliefs and behaviors originate. However, it is probably not too far-fetched to think that the use of eating to help one feel better in part may come from infancy and early childhood. As parents, we are very concerned about our children, especially when they are infants. When an infant cries, we typically go through a short check list. If the baby has a clean, dry diaper and is not in any obvious physical discomfort, we often assume she is hungry and we feed her or at least put a pacifier in her mouth. It is the beginning of an association between feeling and feeding—an association that is carried into childhood. In childhood, we may console our children by giving them something to eat—often a sweet treat—after experiencing the physical pain of an accident or a painful visit to the dentist or doctor or the emotional pain of a personal or social disappointment. Unfortunately, this pairing of emotion and eating may set up a mode of responding in which the individual will use food as a way to console herself for the rest of her life or at least until she is helped to break it.

A disclaimer should be mentioned here regarding fault, blame, or responsibility. The previous paragraph is in no way intended to blame parents or have them feel responsible for their daughter's eating disorder. In their attempts to be as good a parent as they can be, parents may inadvertently use food to help their children feel better. Parents who are working simply to help their children feel better and happier cannot be faulted.

---

## Are There Problem Beliefs
## Held by Most Bulimics
## That Are Not Focused on Food Alone?

Yes. Many bulimic beliefs focus more on the individual's self-worth than on her eating. One list has been compiled by Root, Fallon, and Friedrich (1986). A selection from their work includes the following commonly held thoughts:

### "I Must Be Approved Of by Everyone
### for Everything I Do."

This first belief very much relates to the bulimic's perfectionism and need to please. Her self-esteem is usually related to how others respond to her. She feels that she must please in order to be accepted, approved of, and loved. In actuality, her need to please is probably due more to fear of rejection or abandonment. She feels she is less apt to end up alone if she pleases, and she believes that everyone will be pleased with her if she is perfect. Obviously, there are several difficulties with the bulimic's reasoning. First, she cannot please everyone and thus cannot be approved by everyone. Second, she cannot be perfect. Third, anything less than perfect is unacceptable due to her all-or-nothing mode of thinking.

### "I Should Be in Control and Competent at All Times."

This belief is similar to the first in that it too smacks of perfectionism. Obviously, only a perfect person could always be poised and controlled while being good at everything all of the time. Also, there is an implicit assumption that being in control is always good. Bulimia is a control disorder, and the bulimic frequently feels out of control. There are problems with her conception of control. Control for her too often means she is depriving herself—that she is in control if she does not eat. Unfortunately, control often means that she is not letting her emotions out—that she does not allow herself to be angry with anyone. Her control is all or nothing. Sometimes her control is so tight and restrictive that bingeing and purging are her only release and relief.

### "If Things Do Not Go as I Have Planned, I Am Out of Control"

Again, the issue of control is apparent. When things do not go as the bulimic would like, she assumes she has done something wrong and is out of control; this sense of being out of control is especially apt to occur with regard to eating. She often has difficulty making a distinction between *herself* and feeling out of control and *things* being out of *her* control. Unfortunately, when she feels out of control, she is apt to engage in bulimic behaviors. Bulimics believe that bingeing is out-of-control behavior. We believe, however, that bingeing and purging are attempts on their part to restore a sense of control in that these behaviors are predictable; that is, the individual knows what will happen. Predictability feels like security to her and thus helps her feel more in control.

## "Bulimia is Just a Phase and Will Pass."

This belief is interesting in that it changes over time. In the early stages of bulimia, it is used as a form of denial. By telling herself that it is a phase, the bulimic is also telling herself that she does not need to worry or do anything about it because it will take care of itself as time passes. However, after the individual has been bulimic for a period of time, she comes to believe that it is permanent, that she will never get over it. Obviously, believing either the "phase" or "permanent" premise inhibits recovery. The role of the family or friend regarding this belief is to help her challenge the validity of the belief. Remind her that bulimia is not a phase; it is not simply something you grow out of. The terrible twos is a phase. Adolescence is a phase. Bulimia is a *disorder*. It must be treated in an effort to overcome it.

## "If People Really Knew Me, They Would Think that I Was a Terrible, Weak, Uninteresting Person."

The bulimic has such low self-esteem that she believes no one could really like her. Consequently, when others respond positively, she thinks that they simply do not know her; that if they did know her, they could not possibly like her. This bulimic belief relates to the earlier ones concerning approval, control, and competence. She feels she must always appear to be in control and very competent so as not to give any suspicion that she is not what she appears to be. More specifically, she constantly fears that she will be found out, that she is a fraud.

## "If Anything Goes Wrong, It Is My Fault."

Again, the issue here relates to low self-esteem. Her esteem is so low and she has such negative feelings about herself that she is more than willing to attribute any difficulty, mistake, or wrong-doing to herself. These attributions are consistent with low self-esteem; that is, they fit for her. Therefore, they are quickly and easily integrated into her self-esteem. On the other hand, positive occurrences are typically not attributed to herself; these do not fit with low self-esteem and are not easily integrated. In fact, she will try to explain them in ways that have nothing to do with her. An example is provided by the patient who attributed her excellent grades not to her effort and intelligence, but to the fact that her courses were easy and that her teachers liked her; the latter part about her teachers liking her was quickly dismissed by saying that they did not really know her, that she was fooling them, and that if they really knew her, they would not like her.

## "I Should Be Productive at All Times."

This belief relates to her need for acceptance, approval, and love. She believes that she must be doing something productive in order to have worth—that others will not accept, approve, and love her if she does not do enough things well enough to please them. Again, the real fear here is one of rejection, abandonment, and being alone. This need to be productive relates to how she has lived her life. She has usually spent much of her life doing things in order to please (or at least not displease) significant people in her life. Unfortunately, significant others reward her for what she accomplishes. The young woman begins to think that what she does determines what others think of her. "Doing" becomes her way of obtaining the little bit of esteem and good feeling she occasionally feels.

Also, many bulimics believe they must stay busy in order not to binge. They believe that idle, unproductive time is more apt to lead to binge-eating. To some degree, they are probably right, but not for the reasons they believe. They believe that they have no control over their eating and thus must stay preoccupied doing something else or they will binge. Actually, when not engaged in productive behavior, many bulimics feel restless, guilty, or bored—three feelings they report often lead to bingeing. In essence, she is not bingeing because she is being unproductive but because of how she feels as a result of not being productive.

## What Is Body-Image Distortion?

Body image is the mental picture an individual has of herself. For the eating-disordered person, this body image is distorted in such a way that she misperceives the size and shape of some of her body parts or her entire body. Specifically, she is likely to see herself as larger than she really is. Interestingly, this distortion usually exists only in self-perceptions. That is, she can usually see others accurately, but when she looks at her own body, her perception becomes distorted.

Body-image distortion has many unfortunate consequences. First, it helps her dislike her own body. Second, seeing herself as heavier than she really is makes dieting appear to be more urgent and necessary. And as we discussed earlier, dieting only leads to more bulimic behaviors. Third, it helps her distrust others who tell her she looks great. She assumes they are either lying or that they have undesirable standards. Therefore, eliminating, or at least decreasing, body-image distortion must be an integral part of any treatment program.

## Does Her Thinking Directly Influence
## What or How She Eats?

Yes. Part of the bulimic's irrational thinking relates to misinformation, misconceptions, and myths regarding eating, dieting, and weight. There are numerous myths that many bulimics hold on to and assume to be true. The bulimic's eating is often influenced by these misconceptions. Unfortunately, many of these misconceptions are also held by the public at large, so they are more difficult to identify. Rather than try to cover all the myths regarding eating that are characteristic, we will focus on two of the more frequently occurring myths.

One of the most common misunderstandings involves the relationship between eating and weight gain. Many bulimics (and other people as well) believe that if they eat they will gain weight and if they do not eat they will lose weight. It would be nice if the weight gain and loss process were that simple. Weight gain and weight loss are determined by energy balance — calories ingested versus calories burned. If you eat more than you burn, theoretically you should gain weight. If you burn more than you eat, theoretically you should lose. This sounds simple enough, but it is actually quite complex. Several factors determine energy balance. Age and sex are two such factors that affect metabolism or the rate at which the body burns calories. Basically, the higher or faster the metabolic rate, the easier it is to lose weight, and the lower or slower the metabolic rate, the easier it is to gain weight. Typically, women have a slower metabolism than men, and metabolism usually slows as age increases. More important, metabolism and many other aspects of weight gain and loss, such as set-point weight, are related to genetics and thus are not under the individual's control. Metabolism is also related to eating and exercise. Usually metabolism increases with the frequency and volume of food intake. Conversely, metabolism slows down as frequency and volume of food intake decrease. Exercise tends to raise metabolism as well but may lower metabolism if the individual is underweight and not eating. Additionally, metabolism is sometimes decreased by repeated weight loss/weight gain cycles as a result of dieting.

Another common myth affecting the bulimic's eating involves the notion that all weight gain and loss reflect a gain or loss of body fat. More specifically, the bulimic often believes that she loses fat when she loses weight, which to her is "good." When she gains, she believes it must also be fat so it must be "bad." Again, it would be nice and simple if this were the case; unfortunately, it is not. When weight is lost or gained, it is usually a combination of fat, fluid, and lean muscle mass (sometimes referred to as lean body mass or fat-free tissue). Recent research in the area of weight gain and loss indicates that from one-quarter to one-third of the weight lost due to dieting is lean muscle mass and not fat.

Even when told that the weight she is losing or gaining is not just fat, the bulimic reports she does not care—what she is interested in is what the scales tell her. To her, weight is weight, an increase is "bad" and a decrease is "good." Again, it is not that simple. On the average, 75 percent of the weight gained or lost by most women can be attributed to fat and 25 percent to nonfat tissue. Again, the bulimic might say, "So what?" The real importance here is that the nonfat material they are losing is made up of fluid, protein, and minerals—all of which are vital for good health.

While these are only two of the many myths that many bulimics hold, they greatly influence their thinking and subsequent eating. The way an individual thinks will affect her behavior. Her thoughts and beliefs about food are no exception.

## How Can Someone Change the Way They Think?

Changing the way one thinks is actually easier for many people than changing their behaviors or feelings. Yet when an individual does change her thinking, it then makes changes in what she does and how she feels easier to bring about.

The main strategy in changing thinking is first to learn to identify irrational thoughts or rationalizations. There are many good cognitive treatment books that go into detail about how to identify those thoughts. One we often recommend is *Feeling Good* by Dr. David Burns. Once people begin to recognize their own irrational thoughts and rationalizations, they can then learn how to "talk back" to them and replace them with more rational thinking. Many of our patients write their irrational thoughts and then rewrite them into rational statements. We review this exercise with them within the therapy session, and they are able to make this transition in thinking in a relatively short time frame. When they do alter their thinking, the stage has been set for changes at the behavioral and emotional levels.

## How Can We Help?

1.  Help her rebut irrational statements. The first step in accomplishing this is *awareness,* that is, being aware of when she is using any irrational statements. But a first step in increasing her awareness is for *you* to be aware. This is easier when she is making statements regarding her weight, appearance, and eating because these are observable—you can see the irrationality. For example, the bulimic is forever saying, "I am too

fat." Telling her she is not fat will probably not be helpful; in fact, it may irritate her. Ask her to entertain the notion that she might believe she is fat when in fact she is not. Gently and sensitively remind her that due to being bulimic, her perceptions of and beliefs about herself are probably not totally accurate; and that because her perceptions and beliefs might not be accurate, perhaps focusing on how she is feeling might be more helpful.

Because much of the bulimic's irrational thinking is related to her eating, perhaps an example using eating would be helpful. When she remarks that she cannot control her eating, remind her of the times she has—especially recently. The bulimic individual is much like anyone else who is depressed or has low self-esteem in the sense that she pays much more attention to her mistakes than to her successes. She also assumes that others will also focus only on her mistakes and failures.

As difficult as it is to help the bulimic be aware of her rationalizations and cognitive distortions regarding observable phenomena like weight and eating, it is even more difficult with less observable and more general thoughts regarding who she is. A common way of thinking involves her feeling like a failure because she is not perfect, and her eating disorder becomes a constant reminder of her imperfection. When you hear someone verbalize that kind of thinking, gently question the logic of her thoughts. If she is willing to examine the sequence of her thoughts, she may be able to see the irrationality of her thoughts.

2. Help her when she makes a mistake (binges and purges) with her eating. The damage is usually done *after* the eating mistake. The bulimic's tendency is to berate herself for having been such an "awful" person. These self-statements are, of course, irrational in that she is not an awful person even though she may feel that she is. These statements are not only very destructive psychologically, they also tend to lead to more bingeing and purging. If you are aware of her having made a mistake with her eating, try to help her see that she has simply made a mistake, that we all make mistakes; we don't like having made them and we hope not to repeat them again.

If she can accept this more rational statement, perhaps she will not allow the mistake to lead to subsequent mistakes. Unless she views the first binge and purge episode as simply having made a mistake, the probability of additional episodes is increased. Helping her stop after the first binge and purge episode will be immeasurably therapeutic for her.

3.  Help her plan ahead for difficult situations. The bulimic individual is often faced with situations she finds difficult, such as dinner parties, dinner dates, holidays like Thanksgiving and Christmas, and many other occasions with either family or friends in which food is available. It is easy for her to make negative statements to herself at these times. If she can plan ahead as to what she can do and say to herself (e.g., some pre-planned positive self-statements), it may be easier for her to handle these situations. Equally important is planning for how she might handle possible mistakes or comments by others. As she plans for each contingency, she can feel more in control and therefore feel more at ease.

4.  Challenge her beliefs about food. Most patients we see simply have bad information about food. In order to challenge her beliefs, however, you have to have accurate information. When you hear her espouse a strong belief about eating or weight, go to an appropriate source for the information you need to determine whether her belief is a truth or a myth. This can be done by obtaining books from the library or information from the American Dietetic Association. You could also contact a dietitian at your local hospital for information about different foods and food groups. After obtaining the appropriate information, gently approach her saying you were curious about some of her beliefs about food and you have resources she might be interested in. Simply offer her the information. Do *not* make it a battle or confrontation in which you need to convince her of her errors. She will need time to assimilate the new information and change her beliefs at her own time and pace. You might even suggest she do her own research if she does not believe the information you have found.

5.  Challenge her body-image distortion. When she makes comments about her body size and they seem distorted to you, ask

her if she is willing to test the accuracy of her perceptions. In our office, we do this by using the "rope trick." We have a one-quarter inch thick rope that is about four feet long. We lay the rope in a straight line either on the floor or a table. Then we ask the patient to move the rope into a circle that she thinks accurately reflects the size of her waist. After she has completed that task, we mark the spot and then ask her to put the rope around her waist. We then mark her actual waist size. Individuals with body-image distortion will typically overestimate their waist size. We then put the rope back on the table or floor and show her both her estimated and then her actual waist size. A similar procedure can be used to provide accurate feedback about her hip size as well as other body parts. The impact of this visual and concrete feedback can be very powerful. Then she can begin to learn that she does have a body-image distortion and that it is a function of her disorder. This realization can make it easier for her to "talk back" when she sees herself as fat, or at least to remind herself that she does not perceive herself accurately.

6. Try not to blame yourself if your attempts to help change the thinking of your bulimic friend or family member are less than successful. Changing someone's thinking can be a difficult task even for a therapist who has been trained in this area. Nonetheless, part of the problem may be that the bulimic individual often does not give you enough credibility to help her; that is, she assumes that she knows more about eating than you do or that you do not understand so why should she listen to you. Or, she may have issues with you that make accepting help from you difficult. On the other hand, the therapist is often viewed by the individual as an expert and is more apt to be listened to. This can be perplexing for friends or family members who want to be helpful. They sometimes wonder why the bulimic person would listen to a stranger (therapist) rather than to someone who has known her longer.

# 7

# Emotions

T HE emotional or "affective" part of bulimia is probably the most important; it is also the most difficult and usually the slowest to change.

## How Is Bulimia Related to Feelings?

When most people think of bulimia, they probably think first of the bingeing and purging. In actuality, bulimia is an emotional disorder in which the primary symptoms are bingeing and purging. Specifically, it is a disorder that is used by the individual to help deal with her feelings. Bulimia affects, and is affected by, how she feels, especially how she feels about herself. Generally, the bulimic individual has never learned how to deal with her feelings, especially so-called negative feelings, such as anger, depression, anxiety, and fear.

The bulimic individual is often reared in a family in which emotional expression is neither modeled nor encouraged; in some cases it is even discouraged. Unfortunately, feelings do not leave the person unless expressed in some way. Bingeing and purging distract her from how she feels. Specifically, when she becomes aware of an uncomfortable feeling, she distracts herself with obsessive thoughts of food. These thoughts usually lead to bingeing and purging. What began as an uncomfortable feeling soon becomes a thought that is then translated into a behavior. This sequence of feelings, thoughts, and behaviors can take other forms that relate more generally to eating disorders. For example, the individual may be afraid of something significant in her life but lose her emotional focus and begin to obsess about her weight and body as a distraction.

A patient of ours, Julie, was a twenty-four-year-old college graduate. Julie had several issues relating to growing up that she was afraid to deal with, such as living independently from her parents and taking a professional position in her area of training. When considering job interviews, Julie would become anxious and afraid. Rather than deal with these feelings, however, she would be distracted by her "fat" thighs. Her "reasoning" went as follows: "I have gained so much weight in my thighs and hips that I can't wear my interview suits, and I have to have the right clothes for an interview. . . . I have to lose weight because I won't interview at this weight and I won't buy clothes to fit me as big as I am." She would quickly be off and running in the wrong direction — toward dieting. And of course, dieting would eventually lead to bingeing and purging.

The example of Julie illustrates that her *real* issues were her fears and insecurity about running her own life — issues that are actually maturity fears. It also illustrates the bulimic's need to distract herself from these real issues by focusing on weight and dieting. An interesting postscript to Julie's story is that she did not have fat thighs and hips, but she needed to believe she did so as not to face more difficult feelings she felt too inadequate to manage directly.

Unfortunately for Julie and other bulimic individuals, the feelings have not really been resolved, they have only been put away temporarily; at some point, they will re-emerge. When they do, the person again has to resort to indirect means of dealing with them — thus, the cyclical nature of bulimia.

Bulimia itself also brings other uncomfortable feelings to deal with. It usually creates more anger, depression, shame, and guilt in a person who already dislikes herself and feels worthless much of the time. Each time she binges and purges, she becomes angry with herself because she feels like she has lost control and given in to what she may regard as a "disgusting" habit. She may feel weak, helpless, and hopeless. She feels like a failure and believes she is an awful person and will never change. In essence, the process she uses to manage her emotions simply creates more negative feelings for her to deal with.

Although bulimia does not really take care of feelings and actually creates more uncomfortable feelings to deal with, it does "work" in a sense. If it did not, there would not be so many individuals with the problem and so much resistance to giving up the problem. The term "work" needs some clarification, however. It works in the sense that it is helpful, albeit temporarily. The individual is able to escape her uncomfortable feelings. Using Julie again as an example, we can see how her obsessions about her body and dieting protected her from her feelings of insecurity and immaturity. More specifically, without the "right" body, she could not wear the "right" clothes; without the "right" clothes, she could not get the job that could lead to her independence and the running of her own life. Julie was really afraid she could not get the job or that she could not be successful at the job if she got it. She further questioned whether she could function effectively without her parents making decisions and taking responsibility for her.

Bingeing and purging also provide a release of pent-up emotion. The person's almost constant attempts to maintain tight control create considerable tension and pressure. Bingeing and purging afford the individual temporary relief of some of this tension. Any behavior that reduces anxiety, tension, and pressure will be quickly reinforced through tension reduction; that is, the behavior is followed by a pleasant state of affairs, which means this behavior will be quickly and strongly stamped in.

The use of bingeing and purging for releasing tension is best demonstrated by the case of Kelly, an eighteen-year-old college freshman. Kelly was perhaps the most perfectionistic and compulsive individual we have worked with. During the week, she was engaged in academic work (in class or studying) a minimum of sixteen hours each day. She would lock herself away in her room and force herself to study; she did not have friends over nor watch TV; she would often withhold food until a certain volume of work was done to her satisfaction. On some occasions when she got out of bed in the morning, Kelly would not allow herself to shower, to brush her teeth, or even to go to the bathroom until a certain quantity of work had been successfully completed. Obviously, this lifestyle, when teamed with restrictive dieting, created tremendous tension. This was her life from Sunday evening until Friday evening. Of course, by Friday evening she was as tense and tight as she could possibly be. Her only means of tension reduction was bingeing and purging. Although it was only temporary, the release and relief she felt as a result of bingeing and purging actually made her feel better physically and emotionally. This made getting well difficult because bulimia was the only part of her life that allowed her to let go of the tight, restrictive control that ruled her life.

Perhaps the best way to understand bulimia and how it is related to feelings and tension reduction is to think about a situation in which you have felt angry, anxious, afraid, depressed, disappointed, hurt, and out of control. In that situation, you probably felt bad enough to do almost anything that would help you feel better. As you think about that situation, you may recall that you did in fact engage in some unusual behavior — something that perhaps did not make any sense to anyone else but was somehow helpful to you. This is what the bulimic individual is doing. She has discovered that when she feels bad, she can let go of her usual tight control and let herself binge and purge, which temporarily gives her an escape and some relief from her feelings. There is one difference in your situation and how the bulimic individual lives her life, however. Yours was probably situational and time-limited, while hers is continuous.

## Why Does She Not Know How to Deal with Her Feelings?

We have already mentioned that the bulimic usually grows up in a family in which direct expression of emotion is neither practiced nor encouraged. In addition, we have discussed her need to please those around her in order to feel accepted and approved of. Consequently, she will try to hide emotions that might displease significant people in her life. For example, it is very unlikely that she will directly be angry with a distant father whom she desperately needs and wants to get closer to emotionally. Equally unlikely is an adolescent bulimic girl telling her mother, whom she is too close to, that she feels frustrated and controlled by her. However, when feelings go unexpressed, they do not simply go away; they continue to reside in her. At some point, she must deal with them.

Because she is too afraid to express them directly for fear of rejection, she must resort to her indirect means of managing them through bulimia.

Jenny was a high school student who lived with her parents. No one in her family directly expressed any negative emotion. Because no one expressed emotion openly, Jenny assumed it was not acceptable to do so. More explicitly, she and her siblings were told, "We don't raise our voices here," or "Let's not upset your father." Jenny could also remember an instance when her sister was told by her father, "Don't get angry with me." Consequently, Jenny would try to deny how she felt by telling herself that she was wrong to have the feelings she had, that it was her fault, and that she should do something about it. What she did was binge and purge in an effort to deal with her feelings. If the direct and open expression of emotion had been modeled and encouraged in her family, she most likely could have learned to feel more comfortable about expressing hers. This would perhaps have precluded the need for the indirect means of expression through bulimia.

## Doesn't She Purge in Order Not to Gain Weight? What Do Feelings Have to Do with That?

Bingeing and purging often begin as a misguided attempt to lose weight. The bulimic believes that she will not gain weight if she purges the food she eats. However, usually the longer the individual is bulimic, the more her bingeing and purging generalize to issues other than weight. Although she may continue to use purging to undo eating, bulimia eventually becomes the individual's primary way to deal with emotion.

It must be remembered that many bulimics are not really overweight when they begin to use their purging strategy for losing weight. The fact that she is desperately attempting to lose weight when unnecessary suggests an emotional problem. Also, if the key issue were really weight loss, why would she binge-eat in the first place? This is not to say that most bulimics do not believe they are overweight—they do. This belief, which was discussed in chapter 6, does occur, but the individual's weight and eating are not the problem; rather, they are the symptoms. The bulimic's depression and anger are not primarily a result of her weight and eating (although they contribute), as she believes; her eating and belief that she is overweight are much more often a result of, or a response to, her depression and anger.

## Is Depression Related to Bulimia?

Yes, depression is related to bulimia in several ways. Most bulimic individuals are depressed. As discussed in chapter 4, this depression is sometimes a result of a predisposition to be depressed that can be attributed to heredity; that is, other family members may be depressed and their predisposition to be depressed has been passed on to her. This depression comes from within the individual and is usually due to a biochemical imbalance. This type of depression is often referred to as *endogenous*. The bulimic is usually depressed for psychological reasons as well. This depression, which is related to what goes on outside the individual, is sometimes referred to as *exogenous* or *reactive*. Finally, as described previously, bulimia actually creates more depression for the individual. The relationship between depression and bulimia can probably best be described by the fact that bulimia usually worsens as depression worsens, and vice versa.

Many of our patients believe that they are depressed as a result of how they eat and look, believing the depression to be secondary to, or caused by, their eating and weight. Certainly, once the cycle of depression and bulimia is operating, it is difficult to determine which came first. It is our belief, however, that often the depression precedes the bulimia. This belief is based on several factors. First, when the individual begins to control her eating symptoms, depression is apt to be worse. In fact, what is happening is that she is now more aware of the depression; in essence, the bulimia was distracting her from the depression. Second, when the depression is controlled through appropriate psychological means or medication, the individual usually is better able to decrease her eating symptoms. Finally, many bulimics report their bulimic symptoms to be worse when they feel depressed. Obviously, bulimia is related to depression for many individuals. Attempting to treat the bulimic symptoms without treating the depression would only be dealing with the behavioral part of the problem. The depression—the emotional part of the problem—must be dealt with if the individual is to get well.

## What Is Depression Like for the Bulimic?

Although she is less likely to show it, the depressed bulimic is not radically different from nonbulimic individuals who are depressed. She is unhappy with herself and her life and feels she is helpless with respect to changing this. As a result, she is apt to feel inadequate and inferior. Even though depression is an emotion, it affects more than the emotional part of the person. Behaviorally, she is apt to withdraw socially. In fact, there will likely be a general reduction in activity, with eating and sleeping perhaps being the notable exceptions. Not only is the quantity of activity reduced, the quality of performance also tends to go down when depressed. Her thoughts are apt to be obsessive, confused, and negative, while concentration will be decreased.

## She Seems So Moody. Is That Normal?

Moodiness is certainly not unusual for the bulimic. Her moodiness is related to the fact that she has so many emotions locked up inside her. Her unhappiness and dissatisfaction with herself and her life contribute significantly to her moodiness. When her eating is worse, her mood is apt to be worse. More important, however, her eating becomes worse when her mood is worse.

In discussing personality characteristics in chapter 4, we described the bulimic individual as a very uncertain, ambivalent person who has difficulty making decisions. These characteristics promote a "back and forth," "yes and no" approach to the world, which contributes to her frustration and moodiness. The term "mood" is really suggestive of indirectness; that is, she is not directly angry or openly depressed; she is "moody."

Moodiness may also be related to eating or the lack thereof. Restrictive dieting often leads to an irritability that contributes to moodiness. Dysfunctional eating may also contribute indirectly through low or high blood sugar levels.

Moodiness can also be a result of how the bulimic feels emotionally after a binge and purge episode — guilty, depressed, angry, embarrassed, and frustrated — a sense that she has again failed to be "normal." Peggy, a twenty-four-year-old woman from a very high-achieving family, provides an illustrative example. After bingeing and purging, Peggy would banish herself to her bedroom in an effort to avoid family members. She did not want to talk to anyone, nor did she want anyone to talk to her. If family members tried to help her, she would angrily reject their attempts. At those times, Peggy was so angry with and disappointed in herself that she did not feel she deserved their concern or help. Concern and help from others at that point did not fit with how she was feeling about herself; that is, concern and help were too positive a response to make to such an "awful" person. Additionally, being a part of such a high-achieving family helped her feel embarrassed. When concerned family members tried to help, she felt even more embarrassed. Consequently, it was easier for her to lock herself away and be alone, which her family attributed to moodiness.

In your attempts to be helpful, try to remember that she is not being moody simply to be mean, difficult, uncooperative, or ungrateful. Her moodiness is a communication about how she is feeling. You can use her moodiness to let you know she is having a difficult time. She may or may not want your concern and assistance. The only way to know is to ask her gently and sensitively. If she says "no," honor her answer and let her know you are available if she changes her mind.

On a more positive note, some of the moodiness will dissipate as she becomes more direct with her emotional expression and feels better about herself. Obviously, her moodiness will also dissipate as she gets over bulimia, which is also related to direct emotional expression and increased self-esteem.

## What Other Feelings Are Commonly Related to Bulimia?

Related to the issues of separation, individuation, and attachment discussed in chapter 3, many bulimic individuals have maturity fears that will need to be addressed. *Maturity fears* occur when an individual perceives the responsibilities of adulthood to be too demanding. That is, she finds more security in childhood and psychologically wishes to return to those times when she was taken care of by others. She may fear financially supporting herself; she may fear living on her own; or she may generally fear the idea of taking care of herself. Bulimia becomes one way to manage these maturity fears. If she is too sick to take care of herself, she will not have to face the adult world alone.

## Why Is It So Important to Deal with the Feelings?

While bulimia is a disorder that has behavioral and cognitive components, the feelings are the most important. If we change the individual's eating and her thinking, her problems have not been resolved. We will see the disorder recur or perhaps the emergence of another problem just as debilitating if not more so.

Most bulimics know that their eating is abnormal and unhealthy and should be changed. They can be taught different eating behaviors and how to change other behaviors related to eating. They can even be taught that their thinking is destructive and how it can be changed. Unfortunately, this instruction and the understanding that results from it are not enough. More specifically, the individual can understand where her problem comes from and may know what to do about it, but still be too afraid or too depressed to change her eating. Julie, for example, was able to eat without any bulimic symptoms while she was in the safe, controlled environment of the hospital. However, bingeing and purging would resume quickly and intensely upon release from the hospital. She still knew what to do outside of the hospital; she simply could not do it because of her fear of getting out of control.

There is another reason why emotions are integral in overcoming bulimia. Unfortunately, bulimics are accustomed to people responding to what they *do*. They depend on us to respond to what they do or how they look for the little bit of esteem they can derive from our compliments. This existence is too uncertain and insecure; they feel that they must please or at least that they should not displease in order to feel approved of, accepted, and loved. They really need for us to respond to *who they are* and *how they feel*—they need to be attended to emotionally. They need for us to confirm *them* rather than *what they do.*

We believe that feelings are the most important aspect of bulimia and thus should be the primary focus in treatment. Our belief is based on what our patients have told us regarding the development, maintenance, and treatment of their difficulties. Many have been through treatment that focused primarily on their eating behaviors and were unable to get well; the eating symptoms came back after a period of time. Even those whose behaviors did not return often reported that they still did not like themselves and did not feel in control of their lives. Many of our patients have also told us that they not only preferred an emotional focus but felt it was much more helpful to them.

## When She Begins to Get Well, Will We See a Change in Her Emotional Expression?

One would think that as she controls her bingeing and purging she would feel better. We know that bulimia is used to help her deal with her emotions, that is, to protect her from her feelings by being distracted by the bulimia. In the beginning stages of recovery when she is controlling her bingeing and purging, she usually feels worse because she is no longer being protected or distracted from her feelings. She will feel her depression, anger, anxiety, and all other emotions more intensely. However, now that her feelings are accessible to her, she can learn how to deal with them more directly. It takes a while for her new strategies and procedures to be learned and used. Obviously, this is a critical point in treatment. It is a time in which she is apt to believe treatment is making her worse or that getting better is not worth the effort. This is a time when she will need more encouragement and support from you than perhaps at any other time.

Sandy, a college senior, came to us feeling depressed and confused after three weeks of symptom-free eating. What seemed most frustrating to her was that she expected to feel great once her eating improved. Naturally, she began to question whether treatment was working. In actuality, Sandy had nothing to distract her from her feelings without her bulimia. And without that distraction, she was simply more aware of her depression. We encouraged her to continue with treatment and assured her that we would help her find ways of managing her depression that would be more helpful and less destructive.

## What Can We Do to Help Her with Her Emotions?

1. Express *your* emotions to her. This provides a good model for her and lets her know emotional expression is acceptable. Your emotional expression is especially important with respect to her eating symptoms. When you are afraid, anxious, or angry because her eating upsets you, tell her. Rather than tell her what she should do or not do, express *your* fear for her safety or *your* anger for her irresponsibility, or whatever the feeling is for whatever the issue. It will be less frustrating for her, not to mention more helpful. Also, by expressing your own feelings, you may feel better and have less need to question her about her eating.

   What we have just asked you to do—express your emotions to her—is difficult. Like the bulimic, many of us have not had opportunities to learn how to express emotion openly and directly. Additionally, of all the things that we communicate about, feelings are probably the most difficult. Even for those individuals who are fortunate enough to be adept at emotional expression, it is still difficult. For these reasons, you must be patient with yourself while you are learning, practicing, and refining this new and important skill.

2. Ask her how she *feels*. Too often she is asked about her eating or something else that she has *done*. What she has done refers to *behaviors*. Feelings refer to what is going on *inside* her. Remember, she has not learned how to express her feelings directly, and bulimia often robs her of her feelings—she may not know how she feels. Even if she does not know, she will appreciate your asking. Also, asking will help her learn about her feelings. Sometimes she will anwer with something other than a feeling. For example, bulimics often respond by saying

they feel fat. Fat is *not* a feeling—it may be a sensation, but it is not an emotion. If she responds with something other than a feeling, ask her to translate it into an emotion. It is generally better to let her respond without giving her a choice of emotions. However, if she really is at a loss, it is sometimes helpful to ask if she feels "mad, sad, glad, or scared." Usually, most emotions can be covered by these four, either singularly or in combination. This approach will not only be helpful in getting you the information you need, it will more importantly be helpful to her by increasing her emotional awareness and recognition.

3.  When she expresses her emotions, *listen* and *accept* those feelings. Listening does not simply mean hearing; it is much more. Listen by really attending; attend by remaining quiet and letting her talk; attend by making eye contact when she speaks. Try to listen not only to what she is saying, but also to what she is *not* saying. Emotions are difficult to talk about. More of the emotion may come through what is not being verbalized. *What* a person is saying is often not nearly as important as *how* she is saying it. Listen for the tone, volume, speed, and frequency of speech; these can give us clues about the underlying feelings. For example, if we really listen, we can often hear the tone (light, serious, etc.) of what is being said. An angry person might speak louder, while a fearful person might speak much more softly. An anxious person will probably speak quickly and talk a lot, while a depressed person is apt to speak more slowly and to use fewer words. Be a good listener; good listening is a very facilitative communication that tells her she and her feelings are important.

    In terms of acceptance, we have to be willing to accept whatever she is feeling. If she states that she is depressed, we must accept this. The fact that we see no basis for her depression in no way diminishes the depression she feels. If we respond by saying, "What do you have to be depressed about?" we have not accepted her feelings. If we ask, "Why are you depressed?" our "why" may communicate that she is doing something wrong. Lack of acceptance is what she fears most. Try to remember that feelings are always *real* and *right* even though they may come from *unreal places*. For example, she may report that she is afraid of food. Obviously, food is an inanimate object and as such need not be feared. Nonetheless, her fear is real. She may report being depressed because she is so "fat and ugly." You can look at her and see that she is not really fat and ugly, but her depression is, nonetheless, real.

When someone breaks a leg and the bone is protruding from the skin, it is easy to imagine how painful that might feel. But when someone is feeling depressed, it can be much harder to understand how bad that might feel. The pain of depression, however, can be just as intense as the pain of a fractured leg. The difference is that friends and family often have an easier time empathizing with a compound fracture than empathizing with depression. Depression is much less visible than a fracture and is sometimes difficult to understand. Try and remind yourself that pain is pain, regardless of whether you can see where it comes from.

4. Avoid any cheering-up attempts that deny her feelings. When someone is depressed, there is a tendency for others to want to cheer her up. Sometimes this takes the form of saying, "Things aren't really that bad," "Look on the bright side," or "Others have it worse than you." While this approach is well-intended and may work for a few, most report that it makes them feel angry and frustrated. They believe that you do not understand how bad they feel. Going back to the example of the broken leg, imagine an individual's pain immediately following an accident that resulted in a compound fracture. If someone approaches her and tells her to cheer up and stop feeling sorry for herself because someone else in the same accident lost their leg completely, it is unlikely her pain would go away. While it may be true that others have it worse than she does, this in no way reduces the pain she is experiencing.

Anger and frustration may not be the only feelings evoked by this cheering-up approach. Guilt may also be felt by the bulimic in that this approach may lead her to believe that she has no right to feel bad. Remember, she probably already feels that she is unworthy and undeserving. It is very important that she believes she has a right to feel and to express her emotions.

# Treatment

Treatment is essential because most bulimics are unable to get over this complex disorder on their own. Unfortunately, most bulimics have fears and concerns about treatment that make them apprehensive about seeking the professional assistance they need. Even though most of these fears and concerns are unfounded, they nonetheless affect the bulimic's decisions regarding treatment.

In chapter 8, information and guidance are provided with respect to approaching the reluctant bulimic patient and assisting her into treatment. In addition, various treatment options are discussed. Chapter 9 deals more specifically with what treatment is apt to be like and discusses common issues and problems that may arise in treatment as well as how these might best be managed.

# 8

# Getting into Treatment

## How Do I Approach Her about Treatment?

As has been discussed numerous times in this book, women with eating disorders have a strong need to be perfect and a fear of displeasing others, which make admitting they need treatment very difficult. Additionally, they usually assume that treatment means they will be forced to eat, resulting in weight gain, a condition that they also fear. Consequently, the subject of treatment must be approached with great care and sensitivity. The best strategy is to focus on your concern for her—how she feels both physically and emotionally. You might remark that she appears down or depressed or that she seems tense and irritable. You might comment on her observable symptoms such as sleep difficulty or hyperactivity.

It is probably best that you not talk with her about her eating or weight. There are several reasons for this. First, she is apt to be more threatened and thus more defensive and resistant. Second, it is easier for her to deny that her eating or weight is a problem than it is for her to deny how she feels. Third, she probably thinks about her eating most of her day, making eating and weight very boring and redundant topics.

If she will confide in you that there is a problem, very gently suggest that she (or you and she) seek professional assistance. If she is hesitant, suggest that she seek an evaluation to determine *if* she has a problem. She may be more apt to seek an evaluation than therapy. If she does not accept the referral, it is best not to push too hard at that point unless it is believed that she is at risk medically. After a short period, approach her again with the same concern and sensitivity. If she refuses again, try to hold anger and confrontation in abeyance as long as is feasible. Being overly angry or coercive is apt to increase her fear and need to resist. If you push too hard too soon, one of two negative reactions is likely: she will either push back or be pushed away.

At whatever point she will accept a referral, encourage her to make an appointment at that time because she is likely to change her mind if given enough time, due to her ambivalence about treatment. A referral is always better and is more apt to be taken if the referral is to a specific person; that is, give her a name of a therapist who is knowledgeable and experienced in working with eating disorders. If she is amenable to seeing a therapist but is too afraid to go to her appointment alone, accompany her. Depending on the therapist and the needs and wants of the patient, you may or may not be asked to participate in this initial session.

## What Should We Do If She Denies Having a Problem?

This is a possible response, though many are actually relieved when they no longer have to hide their "secret." If she denies having a problem, there is, of course, the chance she does *not* have a problem. Actually, a bulimic individual knows that her eating is abnormal. Her denial is much more apt to be a defense against admitting to someone else that she is not perfect. Nonetheless, the question of whether she has a problem can be answered if she is willing to have an evaluation. Encourage her to have the evaluation. If she denies having a problem and refuses an evaluation, it is best to simply express your concern and back away. Let her know you are available should she desire to talk with you at a later date.

## Should We, as Friends, Tell Her Family about Her Problem?

Because each case is different, there are no hard and fast guidelines to offer in this regard. Nonetheless, the age of the bulimic individual and the seriousness of the problem should be taken into consideration. In the case of a younger adolescent, encourage her to talk with her parents or school counselor. If she is amenable to this, it is probably best to become less involved at that point and function primarily as a supportive friend. If she is unwilling to talk with her parents or counselor, your decision regarding telling her parents should be based on how she is doing. If you determine she is not in danger at that time, it is probably better to give her more time. Back away and talk with her later. If the individual is older, and especially if she is on her own, it is advisable to encourage her to talk with someone she is close to and to seek treatment. You might also offer to assist her in obtaining information regarding treatment.

When the problem is judged by you to be serious or severe (i.e., physical health is compromised due to excessive purging, self-destructive threats or gestures have been made), more immediate action is warranted. In this case, the individual, regardless of age, obviously needs to be in treatment. She should be told this and be told that you will do whatever is necessary to help get her into treatment. If she refuses to talk with the people close to her, such as parents or spouse, tell her that you intend to do so. Under these circumstances, there are two things you need to remember. First, with the action you are taking, you are risking angering her to the point that she might end her relationship with you. However, if her health is seriously jeopardized, then this risk is worth taking. Second, you need to be aware of your limitations in a situation like this. Even if family members are informed, they may choose to do nothing or be unable to do anything. It is unlikely that the patient, especially one who is eighteen years old or older, can be forced into treatment. And even in the unlikely event that she is forced into treatment, she does not have to cooperate with treatment.

The question of whether her condition is serious enough to

warrant a more active role on your part is always difficult to answer. It is advisable to contact a mental health professional in your area for guidance in this regard.

## What Should We Do If She Refuses Treatment?

If she admits having a problem but refuses treatment, talk with her about her concerns regarding treatment. It may be that you can reassure her that her concerns can be dealt with. Frequently, treatment is refused because the potential patient feels too embarrassed and ashamed to tell another person about her "disgusting habit." Try to reassure her that the therapist will not judge her, that the therapist's job is to be accepting and understanding. If necessary, assure her that the therapist has certainly "heard everything" and will not be shocked by what she has to say.

The bulimic person may refuse treatment, stating that she cannot afford it. First of all, reassure her that she and her health are worth whatever treatment costs and that you are willing to assist her in getting into treatment. Ask her if she has insurance. Some insurance policies will cover at least part of the treatment cost. Suggest to her that some practitioners and public agencies charge for services on a sliding scale, that is, whatever the patient can afford to pay. Offer to help her find such a person or agency. If you are financially able to assist her, discuss the possibility of giving or loaning her some of the money necessary for treatment. If you are unable to help in this way, you can offer to help her find other sources through which to finance her treatment.

In addition to attempting to obtain the finances necessary for treatment, you might take a practical approach and suggest to her how expensive her bulimia is. She may be spending large amounts of money on food, laxatives, diuretics, and medical expenses related to her disorder. Or she may be losing money as a result of missing work due either directly or indirectly to her bulimia. In the long run, her bulimia may cost her much more than her treatment.

Finally, indicate to her that you understand that she feels she cannot afford to be in treatment. But also indicate to her that due to the potential psychological and physiological harm bulimia can do, she cannot afford *not* to be in treatment.

Some individuals refuse treatment because they are afraid they are "crazy" and that being in treatment will only confirm this. Reassure her that bulimia is not craziness. It is true that some of the behaviors involved with it look crazy, but one can engage in crazy-looking behaviors without being crazy. Suggest to her that bulimia looks crazy because it is so difficult to understand and that it feels like craziness sometimes because it is so difficult to control. Indicate to her that treatment can reduce this sense of craziness by helping her understand and control her bulimia.

The bulimic typically feels like a failure and fears that she will not get well in treatment, again proving that she is in fact a failure. First, try to reassure her that most bulimics do get well. Second, suggest to her that she simply work in treatment as long as it takes for her to get well. And finally, encourage her to take the risk of treatment because her risk of failure is not nearly as great as the risk she runs by not being in treatment.

Probably the most frequently used reasons for refusing treatment involve misconceptions about treatment—misconceptions that scare her. For the bulimic, these often concern eating. She is afraid that treatment means she will have to eat. Thus, treatment means to her that she will get fat—the thing she fears most. Suggest to her that treatment does not mean she has to eat; rather, it means she will receive help with her eating, as well as assistance in dealing with her fears, especially those that relate to being fat. Reassure her that her fear and anxiety about treatment simply indicate how important it is.

In the previous paragraphs, we have discussed numerous reasons why the bulimic individual might refuse treatment. We have also discussed several strategies for dealing with these. It may be that you try everything we suggested without positive results. If this is the case, it is advisable to back away for a while. Remember, we do not want to push so hard that we push her away. Give her some time to think about what you have said. After a few weeks, approach her again.

Finally, the reality of making referrals is that many, if not most, referrals are not taken. This is the case for most disorders, but it is especially so for eating disorders due to the needs and characteristics of this group of individuals. Even though you take all of our suggestions regarding referrals and do an excellent job making the referral, she may not take it.

## How Do We Find the Right Therapist for Her?

Finding the right therapist is always important and sometimes difficult. "Right" in terms of qualifications means a therapist who has extensive knowledge of and experience with eating disorders. When contacting a therapist, do not be afraid to ask about experience and success in working with bulimia. If the therapist seems to object, then he or she is probably not a good choice. Your local mental health association may be of help in terms of a referral. There are also regional and national clearinghouses that provide referral information (see Appendix).

"Right" in terms of the right type of person is more difficult. We believe that the right therapy practiced by the therapist is important, but we believe that the right person administering the therapy is probably more important (Thompson & Sherman, 1989). Obviously, the more comfortable the patient can be with the therapist, the more easily trust can be facilitated. However, comfort and trust tend not to occur quickly, so it is important that the eating-disordered individual give the therapist adequate time to create a positive treatment environment. If after a reasonable period of time, the bulimic does not believe her treatment is going well, she should discuss this with her therapist; perhaps a therapist transfer is in order. Do not be afraid to "therapist shop"; it is important that the patient believe she can work well with her therapist.

## What Kinds of Treatment Are Available?

Treatment can be provided in the form of individual therapy, family therapy, and group therapy. Other helpful adjuncts to treatment might include self-help groups, nutritional counseling, and drug therapy. In individual psychotherapy, the therapist is working solely with the bulimic person in an effort to determine how the eating difficulties have developed and how they might be effectively changed and to begin the change process. Although many bulimics engage in the same behaviors, each person is unique and requires a treatment approach that is specifically tailored to meet her needs. Individual therapy provides for this specialized approach.

Family therapy involves not only the bulimic individual but also family members who in some way play a role in her difficulties. Bulimia almost always begins at home. Thus, there are typically interactions or dynamics operating within the family that are maintaining the bulimia. The focus in family therapy is less on the bulimic individual and more on the family as a unit. The goal of therapy is to modify maladaptive family interactions or dynamics through the cooperation and assistance of family members. If these modifications are successfully completed, the need for bulimia by the individual and in the family should diminish.

Of all treatment modalities, group therapy has probably been the most effective in producing therapeutic change. By group therapy, we are referring to a group comprised of eating-disordered individuals, the majority of whom are bulimics, whose primary focus is on issues pertinent to bulimics. Group treatment is beneficial in several ways. First, it allows each individual to discover that she is not the only one with this problem. Second, it provides the bulimic with a group of supporters who will understand how she feels. Third, it gives her a safe environment in which to learn new skills she will need in order to give up her eating symptoms. Fourth, group therapy affords the individual an opportunity to learn from other group members, as well as from the therapist. And finally, the group provides each member with the opportunity to make significant attachments within the group and therapeutic separations at the group's end.

A bulimia self-help group is similar to the therapy group in some respects and quite different in others. The self-help group is actually a support group rather than a therapy group. Whereas the therapy group's goal is to promote therapeutic change, the goal of the self-help group is to provide the support and encouragement necessary to follow through with and maintain therapeutic change. As the name implies, the self-help group is not led by a therapist but rather by a recovering bulimic, or the group may be leaderless. Self-help or support groups are also sometimes available for parents and friends of the bulimic. In most cases, self-help or support groups are free.

Nutritional counseling is usually provided by a registered dietitian and typically involves not only the dispensing of nutritional information but also meal planning. Many bulimics do not believe they need information on nutrition. They assume that they know what they need to eat but simply cannot do it. In actuality, their knowledge of nutrition is often built around calorie counting and myths regarding eating and weight loss. They are frequently surprised to discover how little they know and that much of what they believed has no basis in fact.

Many bulimics have not eaten normally for so long that they do not know how or what to eat in order to eat normally. Through meal planning, the bulimic patient is provided with an eating structure that is tailored to her particular difficulties and goals. This structure not only helps her know when and what to eat but also helps her begin to normalize her eating again. Having an eating plan also reduces some of the bulimic's anxiety and fear associated with eating. Although some patients initially dislike and resist meal planning, many eventually report that it was one of the most helpful aspects of their treatment.

Drug therapy involves the use of medication—typically antidepressant medication, since many bulimics are depressed. This aspect of treatment will be discussed in chapter 9.

As effective as each of the aforementioned treatment methods and adjuncts can be when employed singularly, they tend to produce even greater therapeutic change when utilized together in a multimodal treatment program.

## What Is a Twelve-Step Treatment Approach?

This treatment approach comes from an addictions model such as Alcoholics Anonymous, Narcotics Anonymous, or Overeaters Anonymous. Basically, this approach views alcoholism, drugs, overeating, and so on, as diseases that are lifelong and not curable—they can only be arrested. In other words, "once an alcoholic, always an alcoholic." The twelve-step approach has been immensely valuable in the treatment of alcohol and drug addictions and is probably the treatment of choice for these problems. Unfortunately, this approach has not been very helpful in the treatment of bulimia. More important, we believe that in some respects it is antitherapeutic. Bulimics cannot stay away from food completely the way alcoholics can abstain from alcohol. We need food to live, and it is not helpful for the bulimic to be afraid of food. In addition, there is no evidence to indicate that addiction to foods occurs in the same way that individuals become physiologically addicted to alcohol and drugs. Because Overeaters Anonymous (OA) follows a twelve-step philosophy, we recommend that bulimics avoid that group as a treatment option. While they may benefit from the group support offered in OA, they will also be taught that they cannot control themselves around certain foods, that some foods are addicting and should be avoided, and that they will always have a problem battling food—concepts that we believe are detrimental to the bulimic's recovery.

## Should the Bulimic Be in the Hospital for Treatment?

Hospitalization is always a treatment option—sometimes it is the best option. When the individual's health has been severely compromised, she needs to be in the hospital. When her bingeing and purging are intense, excessive, and out of control, she needs to be in the hospital. At the same time, if the individual is not experiencing either of the aforementioned conditions, it is probably better for her to be treated on an outpatient basis. As explained earlier, bulimia is a control disorder. If we want to assist the bulimic individual to become more in control of her eating, her emotions, and her life, the hospital is not the optimal choice. The hospital takes her control away; the hospital provides the control. Obviously, this is not the ideal way to teach her how to be in control.

# 9

# Being in Treatment

## What Happens in Treatment?

Treatment can be as different and variable as the therapist, agency, program, or hospital providing it. Nonetheless, there are aspects of treatment we feel are necessary if treatment is to be successful. Generally, treatment should address the behavioral, cognitive, and emotional components of the eating disorder. More specifically, treatment goals in the behavioral realm would, of course, require significant reduction of binge and purge behaviors. They should also include the reduction of other compulsive behaviors related to weight and eating, such as dieting, calorie counting, weighing, and overexercising. Treatment would also need to involve the relearning of more normal eating behaviors. Finally, meal planning and dietary instruction to provide a structure and information necessary for normal eating, as well as to undo the eating myths and misconceptions most bulimics operate under, would be integral to making therapeutic behavioral changes.

Treatment goals in the cognitive realm would of necessity include reducing body disparagement, dissatisfaction, and distortion. The patient must be taught to see and think of her body less critically. For example, rather than thinking of herself as being fat, she could be taught to think of herself as not being as thin as she would like—and that she can still be attractive even if she is not as thin as she would like. She could be taught that when she sees herself as being fat this misperception is due to her disorder, and she is not as fat, big, heavy, or ugly as she perceives herself to be. Related to reducing disparagement, dissatisfaction, and distortion would be assisting the bulimic in reestablishing significance in her life. Through society's emphasis on dieting and thinness, she has imbued a thin body with too much significance. She can be assisted in transferring some of this significance to aspects of her life that really are important, such as health, happiness, relationships, school, and job. This transfer allows for a focus away from her body weight. The individual's identity is also related to this area. She cannot get well if she continues to think of herself as a bulimic or as a fat person. She must be taught that she is much more than a body that is judged by how it eats and looks.

Also involved with the cognitive part of bulimia is a need for internal standards by which to make decisions. We have discussed how the bulimic individual typically makes decisions so as not to displease others. In essence, she is using external criteria for deciding what to do. She has practiced this for so long that she has not developed her own standards for guiding her behavior. She should be assisted in determining what she thinks, believes, values, wants, and does not want. She should then be encouraged to act on this internal information to increase her sense of control in her life.

Finally, bulimia is a control disorder, and the individual can be taught to use her thinking to help her feel more in control. She can be assisted in recognizing her use of rationalizations and other cognitive distortions that maintain and exacerbate her eating problem; she can then be taught to restructure her thinking to be more helpful to her.

The affective or emotional part of bulimia is the most important and the most difficult to change. Treatment goals in the affective realm must emphasize increasing direct expression of emotion. As has been described earlier, unexpressed emotion drives bulimia. Emotion must be expressed either directly or indirectly; bulimia is an example of indirect expression. The emotion driving bulimia often consists of the everyday stressors that complicate all our lives. Perhaps more important, however, it is related to underlying issues that often involve the family. An effective treatment program obviously needs to deal with the family and with other underlying issues. Finally, treatment of the affective component would be remiss without continued, concerted efforts to increase the individual's self-esteem, that is, how she feels about herself. No aspect of treatment is more important.

## Does She Need Medical Treatment in Addition to Psychotherapy?

A physical examination is always recommended for any individual who has bulimia. There is a potential for many medical or physical problems that were previously addressed in chapter 1. Although many bulimics do not manifest any physical problems, it is not possible to tell whether or not a problem exists simply by looking. A consultation with a physician is, of course, the best guide. If further medical attention is needed, the physician can advise you in this regard.

Many bulimics resist seeing their physician because they are embarrassed about their disorder. We have been told by countless physicians that many of their patients came for medical problems and never mentioned that they were bulimic. Physicians are not mind readers and most likely will not ask about bulimia unless it is reported to them. Many bulimics also resist seeing their physician because they are uncomfortable having a physical examination. While many individuals are not comfortable having their bodies exposed and examined, this is even more difficult for the bulimic who dislikes her body so intensely.

## Will She Need to Take Medication?

Many bulimic individuals need no medication at all. Others do. Medication may be needed for any physical problems, though this is unlikely. Medication may also be helpful for psychological aspects of the problem—primarily depression. While we do not favor medication for all people who have symptoms of depression, there are some individuals for whom medication will be immensely beneficial. Those individuals who are most likely to benefit from antidepressant medication are those who have a family history of depression or those who have been unable to manage their depression through the psychological approaches that we have referred to throughout this book. If you have questions about the appropriateness of medication, consult with your mental health or eating disorder specialist for a referral to a psychiatrist or physician familiar with bulimia.

## What Are Reasonable Goals to Set?

There is a tendency for the bulimic as well as her family and friends to expect change to occur quickly once treatment has begun. We often have patients and families come to us perplexed when the patient is still bingeing and purging three or four weeks after beginning treatment. It is important to remember that change will not occur immediately for most bulimics. In addition, if unreasonable goals are set up for recovery, the bulimic will simply use this failure as a way to further denigrate herself. "I'm even a failure at treatment," said one patient. Rather than looking for total recovery, try and focus on smaller, more manageable changes. These might include less irritability, less moodiness, fewer comments regarding weight, increased social interaction, more reasonable exercise, less stringent dieting, or a variety of other signs of improvement. Remember, bulimia is much more than simply bingeing and purging. Consequently, improvement involves much more than the elimination of bingeing and purging.

## How Long Will It Take for Her to Get Over This Problem?

It varies with the individual. It could take weeks, months, or more than a year. The duration of treatment is dependent upon several factors. The first and most important is the bulimic's readiness to get well. Even though she wants treatment, she may not be ready. If she has more reasons—both conscious and subconscious—to hold onto her bulimia than she has for giving it up, she is lacking in readiness. This does not mean that she should forego treatment. It simply means the treatment process is apt to take longer because the initial stage will consist of increasing her readiness for change. Second, the time involved is related to how long she has had the problem and how severe the problem is (i.e., bingeing and purging three times daily versus three times weekly). Obviously, the longer she has had the problem and the worse it is, the longer treatment is apt to be. Third, length of treatment can also be related to the personality characteristics of the bulimic mentioned in chapter 4. Some personality types are easier to work with, whereas other types impede or slow down the process. Fourth, treatment is apt to proceed more quickly if the family is involved.

Rather than thinking about how long treatment will take, it is probably more helpful to think of getting over bulimia as a process. It is a process that takes time. It is also a process that is usually uneven rather than smooth. There may be stages in this process in which the patient may feel worse and her bulimic behaviors may actually be increasing instead of decreasing. She may show improvement and then regress. She may appear to be well then relapse. The patient may relapse more than once. What we are suggesting is that treatment should be viewed realistically and rationally but also with patience and cautious optimism. Try not to overreact to the inevitable peaks and valleys in the treatment process.

## Is Exercise Helpful or Harmful to the Bulimic's Chances for Recovery?

Exercise in moderation can be helpful. It is usually viewed as a positive behavior that helps some bulimics feel better physically and psychologically. Exercise can be a positive way to help manage stress and anxiety. It can also be helpful to the depressed bulimic in that it can energize the psyche, as well as the body, and help her restore a sense of control.

Unfortunately, moderation is a difficult concept for most

bulimics, and exercise can quickly become excessive. The bulimic may reason that if running five miles is good then running ten miles must be great. Susan, a patient of ours, provides an illustrative example. Susan very much enjoyed exercise, but once she started it was difficult for her to stop. A planned three-mile run often became five, and a five-mile run frequently became seven or eight. The excessive exercise significantly increased her appetite, which sometimes led to bingeing.

Exercise for the bulimic can also become compulsive in that she feels she *must* exercise. If she does not, she may feel guilty for not doing what she was *supposed* to do, or she may feel anxious that she will gain weight. When compulsive, the patient's entire day may be scheduled around her exercise time. Additionally, exercise can easily become another way to lose weight or to purge, that is, to undo the effects of eating.

As long as the bulimic individual is physically healthy and exercise is not excessive, compulsive, or used as a purgative, it is not only acceptable, it is recommended. However, if the individual experiences anxiety, guilt, or depression when unable to exercise, it should be curtailed or eliminated until these withdrawal effects can be dealt with in treatment.

## Is It Okay to Ask Her about Her Therapy Sessions?

Preferences vary with the individual. One patient of ours felt hurt that her family never asked about her treatment. Another patient felt her family was being too controlling when they questioned her about her treatment. There is really only one way to find out how she feels about discussing her treatment and that is to ask her. Tell her you are concerned about her and are thus interested in how her treatment is going. If she indicates she does not want to discuss her treatment with you, honor her wishes. However, this does not preclude you from inquiring how she is feeling, which is what treatment is about and probably what you are really interested in anyway.

## Can I Talk to Her Therapist?

This is an issue that must be decided by the patient and therapist. Professional ethics regarding confidentiality preclude the therapist from releasing information about the patient without her consent. Even though these ethics do not apply with regard to receiving information about a patient, therapists vary with regard to their willingness to accept information from others about the patient. If the patient is willing to permit her therapist to release information, she will need to authorize this release in writing. It is also helpful to the therapist if the patient can be specific about what information is acceptable to release to what people. Finally, the therapist may choose not to disclose information about the patient even with her consent if the disclosure is deemed not to be helpful to the patient.

## Will Treatment Be Successful? Will She Get Well?

This question is difficult to answer, in part because the answer depends on how "treatment success" or "getting well" are defined. As mentioned earlier, it is probably more helpful to think of treatment in terms of a process rather than in all-or-nothing terms. It is not a situation in which the bulimic will either get well or she won't. She will experience varying levels of improvement at different stages of treatment. She may get to a point at which she has been symptom-free for a long period—a condition that might be called "well." Until she reaches this point, she should be praised for whatever level of improvement she has been able to achieve and be encouraged to continue working at making herself healthier. If she does not improve, praise her efforts and encourage her to keep working.

It is difficult to determine exact figures, but treatment outcome studies, as well as our clinical experience, suggest that approximately 60 percent of bulimics become bulimic symptom-free, approximately 20 percent do not eliminate all symptoms but significantly improve, while 20 percent do not improve in treatment. It goes without saying that the individual must stay in treatment in order to get well. With low frustration tolerance, high needs for achievement and perfection, and a tendency to be impulsive, many bulimics find it difficult to remain in treatment long enough to get well. In fact, the treatment dropout rate for bulimics is much too high. The other conditions that affect treatment success—patient readiness, problem severity and chronicity, personality characteristics, and family involvement—were discussed in a previous section of this chapter.

## What Should We Do If She Drops Out of Treatment?

Try not to be judgmental. Treatment is often threatening, time-consuming, and difficult. She probably has a good reason for dropping out. In a gentle and nonaccusing manner, ask her what is wrong. If she can and will tell you, listen carefully, then offer to assist her with her concerns. The key word here is "assist": do not push.

Many patients drop out of treatment because they do not feel they are making progress. They feel that they are "just wasting time and money" or they are "failing." As was discussed earlier, many bulimics drop out of treatment due to personality characteristics that lead them to be impatient and impulsive. If your bulimic family member or friend has dropped out of treatment because she was not improving as rapidly as she thought she should, remind her that she has had her problem for a long time and it will take some time to overcome it. Tell her that you know bulimia is a difficult problem to get over and that difficult problems take time to resolve. Reassure her that you are not concerned about how long her treatment takes, but rather that she gets well.

Some patients drop out of treatment because of difficulties relating to the therapist or to the other patients if treatment involves group therapy. If she will confide in you that her problem is with the therapist, encourage her to talk with the therapist. Suggest to her that therapists are usually understanding people who really have their patients' welfare at heart, but that they, nonetheless, are not perfect and make mistakes. Indicate to her that talking with the therapist about possible mistakes could be helpful both to her and to the therapist. Even if mistakes have not been made, talking with the therapist about what she likes and does not like about treatment could bring about changes that would make treatment more amenable to her.

If the bulimic's reason for leaving treatment involves other patients, encourage her to go back to group therapy and talk about her difficulties. This is the purpose of group therapy. Remind her that she and the other group members are in treatment because they are bulimic and that bulimia and difficult interpersonal relations sometimes go hand in hand. For some patients who are socially or interpersonally uncomfortable, bulimia may have become a substitute for social interaction. For others, bulimia may interfere with interpersonal relations by creating low self-esteem, frustration, irritability, moodiness, and depression. Also, remind her that many bulimics have great difficulty telling others when they are having problems with them and often leave the unpleasant situation to avoid more bad feelings or confrontation. Encourage her to go back to her group with this understanding and try to work out her concerns within the group. Suggest to her that, by doing so, she not only can resolve the short-term problem in the group but also can make a very positive step in getting over her bulimia.

Sometimes the bulimic will drop out of treatment simply because she is afraid. She may even use the previously mentioned reasons for treatment dropout—not making progress or difficulty with therapist or patients—as excuses when she is afraid. She may be afraid to really let go and talk about what is inside her. Remember, a bulimic person fears letting go of her control and assumes that whatever is inside her is "not good enough." She may fear that family secrets will come out in treatment and cause trouble for her or other family members. She may be afraid that getting well means eating and that eating means she will become fat.

Most important, the bulimic may be afraid to get well. Getting well may mean making changes she either does not want to make or does not believe she can make. These changes are not only those that occur during treatment, but they also are the changes she is expected to make after treatment. One patient told us that she did not want to get well because it meant that she would be expected to do several things she either could not or did not want to do. She believed that her husband would expect her to be "more sexual" with him, which she did not want to do for a variety of reasons. She believed that he would also expect her to both get a job and be a better mother to their children—the former being something she did not want and the latter being something she did not think she could do. She was convinced that her parents would expect her to go back to college, which she neither wanted nor believed she could do. For her, an eating disorder appeared preferable to dealing with the aftermath of getting well.

If she confides in you that she is afraid of getting well, indicate to her that getting well means she will be healthier and happier; it does not mean she has to *do* or *be* anything. It does not mean she has to be a better wife, mother, lover, student, or anything else. Remind her that getting well means she will be making her own decisions about what she wants and does not want. It also means becoming better able to talk and deal with people who are apt to place unrealistic or unwanted expectations on her. Assure her that you do not expect her to be or do something for you when she is well. Finally, convey to her that you accept and understand her fear about getting well but that fear does not mean she cannot or should not get well. Fear simply indicates that getting well is very important.

In our discussion of handling treatment dropout, we have presumed that the patient would be willing to discuss her concerns. In many cases, she may not be so willing. If she is not, the best approach is simply to tell her how concerned you are about her and that you will be available if and when she decides she wants to talk about her treatment concerns.

Finally, it is important to know your limitations in getting your bulimic family member or friend back into treatment. You may do an excellent job of being accepting, understanding, and helpful when talking with her. You may say and do all the right things, and she still may opt not to return to treatment. Should this occur, do not push. Again, be accepting and understanding, and tell her that you do not agree with her decision but that you respect it. Also, let her know that you are willing to be helpful to her in any way you can. Then compliment yourself for having done a difficult job as well as you could do it.

## How Will We Know When She Is Well?

Because we see the problem of bulimia as multifaceted and made up of behavioral, cognitive, and emotional components, we view recovery as reflecting significant change in all three areas. Our criteria for getting well correspond closely to our treatment goals for these three areas, which were discussed in the initial section of this chapter. Please refer to that section.

## Once She Completes Treatment, Will She Be Able to Stay Well, or Will She Have a Relapse When She Is under Stress or Something Goes Wrong?

First, remember that treatment and recovery are processes that occur over time. An isolated binge and purge episode that occurs after several weeks of symptom-free eating may simply be a slight step backward in the recovery process. Certainly, the bulimic is capable of having her symptoms again; in fact, a brief return of a symptom or two may be so much a part of the normal process of recovery that minimal bingeing and purging might be anticipated. An isolated binge and purge episode, however, does not constitute a relapse. Rather, it is simply a mistake and a temporary return to a previous mode of dealing with her life.

The likelihood of a true relapse decreases if she has a plan for handling difficulties. For this reason, relapse prevention training should be a part of any effective treatment program. It is designed to alert the bulimic to potential problem signs and instruct her regarding how best to respond.

The best response often involves a brief return to treatment where an immediate intervention can be undertaken. Unfortunately, the individual often puts off returning to treatment until the bulimia is again out of control. Sometimes she puts off returning to her therapist because she is embarrassed and may feel like she has failed. Also, she will often increase the likelihood of relapse by the negative messages she gives herself. In addition to telling herself that she is a failure, she may believe that she has "ruined everything" that she had accomplished in treatment. She may tell herself that she cannot get well. She may convince herself that she has now "blown it" and that it does not matter how much she binges and purges. If she returns to treatment, she can be reassured that her mistakes are a normal part of recovery and that only perfect eaters do not make mistakes. She can be further reassured that she will probably continue to make mistakes, but that it is how she handles her mistakes that determines whether she will continue to improve.

Many treatment programs also offer aftercare treatment (usually less intensive treatment) following the primary portion of her program, which can be helpful in preventing relapse. The probability of relapse is also less if the individual attends a self-help support group for bulimics. Most cities offer such a group.

## A Final Word

You have just finished reading a book that we hope has increased your understanding of bulimia. If you are a concerned friend or family member of someone who is bulimic, congratulate yourself for your efforts toward helping her deal with this very difficult problem. If you are struggling with bulimia yourself, take solace in the fact that you have at least begun to explore the possibility of getting well. This book, however, is not enough. Treatment is still necessary. It will not be easy, but your hard work and patience will increase the likelihood of it being successful.

# Appendix: Resources

THE following organizations provide a variety of information on bulimia and its treatment. Most provide a list of therapists, doctors, treatment programs, and hospitals that specialize in the treatment of eating disorders. In addition, you can contact your county or state mental health association for local treatment options.

**American Anorexia/Bulimia Association, Inc. (AABA)**
293 Central Park West, Suite 1R
New York, NY 10024
(212) 501–8351
AABA provides a nationwide referral list. It also offers information packets and publishes a newsletter.

**Anorexia Nervosa and Associated Disorders (ANAD)**
P.O. Box 7
Highland Park, IL 60035
(847) 831–3438
ANAD maintains an international referral list of therapists and programs. It also sponsors a national network of support groups. In addition, ANAD has a newsletter and information packets available upon request.

**Anorexia Nervosa and Related Eating Disorders, Inc. (ANRED)**
P.O. Box 5102
Eugene, OR 97405
(541) 344–1144
ANRED offers free information packets and provides an information clearinghouse. They do not make referrals, however.

**Bulimia Anorexia Nervosa Association (BANA) of Canada**
3640 Wells Avenue
Windsor, Ontario, N9C 1T9, CANADA
(519) 253–7421
BANA provides a referral directory for Canada. In addition, they offer a newsletter, a resource library, and information packets.

**National Eating Disorders Organization (NEDO)**
6655 S. Yale Avenue
Tulsa, OK 74136
(918) 481–4044
NEDO maintains an international referral list as well as providing information packets, newsletters, and packets for support groups.

# References

American Psychiatric Association. (1994). *Diagnostic and Statistical Manual of Mental Disorders*, Fourth Edition. Washington, DC: American Psychiatric Association.

Britton, A. (1988, July/August). Thin is out, fit is in. *American Health, 7*, 66–71.

Burns, D. (1980). *Feeling good: The new mood therapy.* New York: William Morrow & Company, Inc.

Fallon, P., Katzman, M. & Wooley, S. (Eds.). (1994). *Feminist perspectives on eating disorders.* New York: The Guilford Press.

Feeling fat in a thin society. (1984, February). *Glamour Magazine*, 198–201, 251–252.

Garner, D.M. & Garfinkel, P.E. (1980). Socio-cultural factors in the development of anorexia nervosa. *Psychological Medicine, 10*, 647–656.

Garner, D.M. Garfinkel, P.E., Schwartz, D. & Thompson, M. (1980). Cultural expectations of thinness in women. *Psychological Reports, 47*, 483–491.

Klesges, R.C. (1983). An analysis of body distortions in a nonpatient population. *International Journal of Eating Disorders, 2*, 35–41.

Louis, D. (1983). *2201 fascinating facts.* New York: Greenwich House.

Metropolitan Insurance Company. (1983). *Metropolitan height and weight tables.* New York: Metropolitan Insurance Company.

Moses, N., Banilivy, M.M. & Lifshitz, F. (1989). Fear of obesity among adolescent girls. *Pediatrics, 83*, 393–398.

Nielson, A.C. (1979). *Who's dieting and why.* Chicago: A.C. Nielson and Co., Research.

Root, M., Fallon, P. & Friedrich, W. (1986). *Bulimia: A systems approach to treatment.* New York: Norton & Company.

Thompson, R.A. & Sherman, R.T. (1989). Therapist errors in treating eating disorders: Relationship and process. *Psychotherapy, 26*, 62–68.

Thompson, R.A. & Sherman, R.T. (1993). *Helping athletes with eating disorders.* Champaign, IL: Human Kinetics Publishers.

25th Swimsuit Issue. (1989, February). *Sports Illustrated, 70*, Time Inc.

Wolf, N. (1991). *The beauty myth: How images of beauty are used against women.* New York: Morrow.

# Index

Schwartz, D., 149
Schwartz, E., 149
Self-destructiveness, 60–61
Self-esteem, 10, 50–51, 64–66,
    98–101, 117–118, 137
Separation, 40–41, 116
Set-point weight, 29, 63, 103
Sherman, 8, 130, 149
Social pressure for thinness, 17–18,
    20–21, 24, 29, 31
Societal standards for attractiveness,
    19–20, 22–27, 32
*Sports Illustrated,* 22–23, 149
Stealing, 59–60, 69–70
Suicide risk, 60–61
Support groups, 14, 131–132, 146

Tension reduction, 8–9, 80–81, 84
    111–112

Thompson, M., 149
Thompson, R., 7, 130, 149
Treatment: dropout, 142–144;
    evaluation, 125–126; goals,
    135–138; modality, 130–132;
    refusal, 128–130; success,
    138–139, 141–142, 145–146

Unrealistic expectations, 29, 42, 53

Vomiting, 3–4, 18, 84–85. *See also*
    Purging

Water pills: *See* Diuretics
Weighing, 81–83
Weight change, 81, 86–87, 102–103
Wolf, 18, 149
Women's movement, 27–29
Wooley, 29, 149

# About the Authors

**Roberta Trattner Sherman,** Ph.D., and **Ron A. Thompson,** Ph.D., are psychologists who founded the Bloomington Center for Counseling and Human Development, a center specializing in the treatment of eating disorders in Bloomington, Indiana. They also developed and now codirect the Eating Disorders Program of Bloomington Hospital. In addition to full-time clinical practice, Drs. Sherman and Thompson lecture, write, and conduct research in the area of eating disorders.